ASIAN STARTUP FAILURES

Lessons and Case Studies for Success

Stephan S. Sunn

Davidson Global & Co.

Copyright © 2024 Stephan S. Sunn

©Copyright 2024 -2027 Stephan S. Sunn All Rights Reserved

Disclaimer:

This book may not be reproduced or transmitted in any form without the written permission of the authors. Every effort has been made to make this guide as complete and accurate as possible. Although the authors have prepared this guide with the greatest of care, and have made every effort to ensure its accuracy, we assume no responsibility or liability for errors, inaccuracies, or omissions. Before you begin, check with the appropriate authorities to ensure compliance with all laws and regulations. Every effort has been made to make this report as complete and accurate as possible. However, there may be mistakes in typography or content. Also, this report contains information on online marketing and technology only up to the publishing date. Therefore, this report should be used as a guide – not as the ultimate source of Internet marketing information. The purpose of this report is to educate. The authors do not warrant that the information contained in this report is fully complete and shall not be responsible for any errors or omissions. The authors shall have neither liability nor responsibility to any person or entity concerning any loss or damage caused or alleged to be caused directly or indirectly by this report, nor do we make any claims or promises of our ability to generate income by using any of this information.

Davidsons Global & Co. LLC, Davidson, NC 28036, USA; All Inquiries of copyrights, and cooperation go to: Stephan.sunn@aya.yale.edu

CONTENTS

Title Page
Copyright
Preface
Chapter 1: Asian Startup Ecosystem
Chapter 2: Cultural and Regulatory Terrain
Chapter 3: Business Model Errors
Chapter 4: Financial and Funding Mismanagement
Chapter 5: Leadership and Team Misplays
Chapter 6: Market Entry and Expansion Blunders
Chapter 7: Product Development and Innovation Faults
Chapter 8: Regulatory Compliance Challenges
Chapter 9: Missteps in Marketing and Sales
Chapter 10: Operational and Supply Lapses
Chapter 11: Cultural and Social Mismatch
Chapter 12: Founder and team Psychology Burdens
Chapter 13: Build Profitable Asian Startups
Acknowledgement
About The Author
Books By This Author

PREFACE

Success stories command the headlines in vibrant Asian entrepreneurship, but some of the best learning can be found in the stories of failure that are largely unremarked. We have spent many years as business advisors and have written numerous research papers and books, observing and recording the successes and setbacks that shape entrepreneurial experiences throughout Asia.

Why focus on failure? In Asian startup ecosystems, where success is celebrated at times and failure may be stigmatized, understanding why ventures fail is the most viable first step toward continued business success. Each chapter in this book represents a multi-year accumulation of hands-on experience and meticulous analyses of several startups that failed. This book will provide pragmatic insight, not theoretical frameworks.

To the fresh lot of young reading this book, be it a fresher or budding entrepreneur or an executive moving around in the jungles of the startup ecosystem, this is for you. Our purpose is to assist you in avoiding common pitfalls, securing better job opportunities, converting your entrepreneurial aspirations into viable businesses, and increasing your market access.

The Asian ecosystem for startups is challenging at many levels from rapidly changing technology with complex regulations to nuances of culture and market fragmentation. Much more than a good idea is needed for it to succeed: it requires understanding, preparation, and, above all, resilience. With this book, we try to open an avenue for the free and honest discussion of failures within Asian business culture. Every successful entrepreneur has setbacks. The only thing different is that they do not let their failure get in the way but instead learn from it and come out even stronger.

Let this book be the practical companion on your entrepreneurial journey that will help you surmount many obstacles, leverage opportunities, and create the future you want. The journey will indeed be arduous, but that can surely lead to some very extraordinary destinations- depending upon the insight one uses.

CHAPTER 1: ASIAN STARTUP ECOSYSTEM

This chapter is going to review the Asian ecosystem for startups, describing its dynamic growth, peculiar features, and challenges that face the emerging company. We analyze reasons for startup failures across selected Asian countries, systematizing internal dynamics and broader Asian business environment issues and country-specific circumstances. This chapter shall attempt to provide insights into the complex and rapidly evolving landscape of Asian entrepreneurship.

The book, therefore, undertakes a detailed investigation into the various kinds of issues that afflict startups in Asia. We decided to focus on a few specific Asian countries and conducted almost a forensic analysis of the reasons for the failure of startups. We categorize these causes under three heads :

- Those coming from within the internal dynamics of the startups
- Those baked into the broader business environment of Asia as a whole
- Those caused by unique political, social, and economic circumstances present in specific countries in Asia

The case studies presented in this book are by no means representatives of a holistic vision of the Asian startup ecosystem but symptomatic of much larger conditions that invalidate the success of less-than-stellar startups across most of contemporary Asia.

A Dynamic Growth in Asian Startup Ecosystems

In the past ten years, Asia has experienced a tremendous upsurge in startup creation. Some of the most creative, go-to destinations for innovation have emerged in the region. In Southeast Asia, a mixed bag of diversity presents a terrific opportunity for scaling startups across several countries—if they can overcome the monumental challenge of dealing with a system of governance that seems to vary (and even contradict itself) from country to country. Meanwhile, East Asia continues to boggle the world with its technology innovations, and in South Asia, with its center of gravity in India, the region has transformed into a gigantic IT market and a surprising center of entrepreneurial activity with promises—from both the region's governments and its entrepreneurs—that they will "go digital."

Taking a broader view of the emergence of an archipelago of ecosystems in the Asian region, this phenomenon appears to be happening on a very large scale and at an almost breathtaking velocity. The venture capital investment numbers tell this part of the story dramatically—more than doubling, tripling, or exploding—from about $6.7 billion in 2013 to over $80 billion in 2023—numbers that simply do not exist anyplace else in the world.

Distinctive Features of the Asian Startup Ecosystem

There are a few main characteristics that define the Asian startup ecosystem.
- Asia is inherently diverse. There is a profusion of languages, cultures, and regulatory environments among the many countries that comprise the continent. This demands localized approaches when it comes to creating and nurturing startups and presents a significant scaling challenge for any business that aspires to operate across the entire region.
- Moreover, a number of Asian countries have quickly embraced the mobile platform and leapfrogged to a mobile-centric society. This has inspired many innovative business models, particularly in the payment and e-commerce spaces, built around the mobile phenomenon.

- Government engagement: The majority of Asian governments are playing a part—often an active one—in the development of their nascent startup ecosystems. They achieve this through a range of policy instruments and by providing various kinds of funding and infrastructure (from co-working spaces to incubators). This is generally taken to be a positive development. But for a venture capitalist, it can also be a mixed blessing: More and more, we're competing not just with one another but also with our own governments for the startup ecosystem's limited resources.
- Swift technology adoption: Many Asian consumers are early adopters of new technologies. Opportunities in "new tech" areas such as AI, blockchain, and IoT are created by technology customers.
- Distinctive Social and Cultural Practices: Heavily social business practices, such as guanxi, have a strong influence on how business throughout Asia is conducted.

The Challenges Faced by Unicorns in Asia

The Asian startup ecosystem is brimming with exceptional companies; however, the situation is not all positive. The problems that these young companies face are hard to solve and may not have solutions at all. If we take a look behind the exhilarating number of mentions in the press, we see a handful of major issues:

1. The vast majority of these startups are still figuring out their business models, many of which seem to be without profit (or a reasonable path to profit) baked in.
2. Finding talent remains a colossal issue; the result is intense competition for a few qualified people and a lot of rapid turnover.
3. And startup after startup is bumping, in its narrative, into cultural and regulatory obstacles that make its Asian business model hard

to replicate in the West.

Learning from Failure

Learning from failure is so important. And we never talk about it enough. Most conversations regarding the topic summarize the dynamics around what made an entrepreneur fail. And though it is good to know "why we fail", that is not very deep. The depth comes when we discuss "how" and "what" fails:

- How do we fail?
- What do we take away from it?

These, I feel, are questions we should be asking more often: not just about startups—considering that their stories are rarely linear—but also in a broader Asian entrepreneurship context.

Key Takeaways

1. The Asian startup ecosystem is a rocket ship sailing to a destination of incredible wealth. Between 2013 and 2023, venture capital investments in that part of the world went from a comparatively modest $6.7 billion to over $80 billion.
2. The Asian startup ecosystem has some unusual features. One is its sheer size, with over 4.5 billion people in the potential customer base—the diverse and largely affluent Asian market. A second is its increasingly mobile-first economy. A third is the involvement of Asian governments, which are funneling new resources into the startup sector.
3. But in the midst of this rocket ship's ascent toward the incredible wealth that plumes in its upper atmosphere, Asian startups still have some serious problems. Their biggest issue is profitability. A close second is finding and keeping the talent they need to grow and scale their businesses.

4. Learning to fail effectively is important. It is a skill that unfortunate but ultimately successful entrepreneurs are developing, and that the Asian startup ecosystem is developing as a whole.

Extended Issues to Address

1. In comparison to other regions like North America and Europe, what are the unique qualities of the Asian startup ecosystem?
2. Asian startups grapple with fragmented markets and assorted, in some cases, conflicting regulations. What are some ways they can push through these obstacles to achieve regional growth?
3. The learning curve for startups in Asia can be steep when lessons from failures are not well integrated into the ecosystem. What can be done to rectify this?
4. Government support in many forms is an important ingredient for a healthy startup ecosystem. What are some ways this support can be rendered without hampering creativity and innovation?

CHAPTER 2: CULTURAL AND REGULATORY TERRAIN

The Asian startup community is woven of an intricate network of different cultures, each with its own business practices and ways of getting things done. If you want to launch a successful startup in Asia, or within any of its many sub-regions, you have to better understand the culturally bound way your business will function. Not to mention that locally or in Asia as a whole, you will always find yourself competing within a multicultural environment. One fundamental aspect of Asian cultures that influences, often deeply, this "inside" or "invisible" way of functioning business is the deference they pay to the group over the individual.

A Business Culture Centered on Relationships

The Asian business culture places intense importance on personal relationships. In China, it's called "guanxi"; in Korea, "inhwa"; and in Japan, "keiretsu." These terms all relate to the significant focus on networking and the personal dimension of business, which plays out in a number of key areas like the sales process and partnerships. There's a saying in the Asian business world: "If you don't have a friend, you won't get to the end." Indeed, the personal commitment and trust that underpin relationships are often covered by the "friendship factor."

When it comes face-to-face with a business in Asia, a Western company is often operating under a different playbook—one that prioritizes reputation, social standing, and managing the public's perception of a company.

The Emphasis on Hierarchy and Risk Aversion within Fragmented Markets

Asian cultures tend to have strong hierarchical structures. This can influence the dynamics of startups, especially in three main areas:

1. Decision-making tends to happen at the top. This can make some startups in Asia very slow to innovate. It also tends to lead to communication structures where people subordinate to the leaders and founders of a startup are very careful in what they say.
2. Talent retention. Many younger people in Asia apparently have some trouble adjusting to the rigid structures that are common in many Asian startups.
3. Risk aversion. Many Asian cultures (and, it's worth noting, some Asian-American cultures) are very conservative about what we might call "entrepreneurial risk."

The regulatory environment in Asia varies as widely as its cultures, which poses a considerable challenge for startups operating across borders. On one side, there is China, which has a tech sector that sees a high level of government involvement (and which is in no way comparable to startups' experiences in places like, and rulemaking that is sometimes so sudden and dramatic as to seem unfriendly. On the other side, there's India, which may be the Wild West in terms of an evolving regulatory framework but whose increasing government focus on data localization and e-commerce rules is a new frontier for most tech startups. In the middle, jurisdictions like Singapore seem to offer a more friendly deal, with a straitlaced tech regulatory environment that's backed by a government that wholeheartedly supports and encourages tech startups.

The fintech financial sector has varied and intricate regulations to navigate. For one, cryptocurrencies are treated very differently from place to place. China's hard ban, for instance, stands in stark contrast to Japan's regulated embrace of the technology. In Southeast Asia, new digital banking licenses are being introduced, creating the potential for exciting innovations in countries like Singapore and Malaysia. But those new opportunities also pose new challenges in terms of what regulations startups will have to follow. Another layer of this regulatory puzzle is made up of employment laws, which can have a big impact on how (and how easily) a startup can staff itself. Japan's embrace of the "lifetime employment" model and China's very structured "hukou" system (which governs where people can live and work) both represent unique challenges for startups considering doing business in those markets.

IP Protection Strategies

- **File Patents and Trademarks Early:** No matter how starry-eyed you may be after your first few elevator pitches, remember that investments in startups are serious business for investors, and they will want to see returns. This means that your IP is probably, if not definitely, the most important part of your innovation that you need to protect. Why? Because once an investor gives you money if they have even the slightest inkling that someone else is infringing on your technology, the whole thing they've bet on becomes worthless. So how do you protect your precious IP?
- **Use Non-Disclosure and Non-Compete Agreements:** You make your employees sign NDAs and NCAs at the very least, but your attorneys probably should too. And then, to be safe, let your attorneys use the agreements to draft even safer agreements (like I've been known to do).

The tech centers in Asia are often likened to Silicon Valley, but there are important differences that set them apart. These centers are home to a rapidly growing venture capital presence. The flap over the Chinese ByteDance's misleading TikTok ads for the election has rekindled talk of regulating the platform in a Freedom of Information Act manner. But at what cost to access? Covering the costs and access issues involved in regulating a tech center's platform would be one way to ensure the tech centers in Asia remain a close second to the business ecosystem found in Silicon Valley.

Silicon Valley is a worldwide talent magnet with a truly global reach and a strong entrepreneurial culture. For a long time, it has attracted talented people from all over the world to make their homes here. But now our Asian competitors are also developing strong local talent pools, and local recruitment challenges are forcing us to think and act more like our Asian competitors when it comes to hiring and retaining the skilled professionals our local startups need in order to be successful and to grow.

Asian startup hubs are developing paths for their own exits, with an initial public offering (IPO) appearing to be the most plausible route. Compared to the robust array of acquisition opportunities present in Silicon Valley, however, our Asian hubs provide nascent firms with fewer avenues to take if they want to liquidate and realize their investments. This impacts the funding and growth strategies many Asian startups choose to pursue.

The Asian centers where I have worked offer a slight contrast to Silicon Valley. They prioritize elegance and practicality over audacity and ambition. I have learned from my colleagues in the Asian offices, including those of you working here with me today, that innovation can take many forms. The Asian path to innovation is often more efficient than the largely hit-or-miss approach characterizing our model on the other side of the Pacific.

Ecosystem Development

Silicon Valley has a long-established, highly developed ecosystem with networks of founders, investors, and mentors who are collaborative and share knowledge. The hubs in Asia are still relatively recent in comparison but are maturing quickly. The support infrastructure varies widely across these different countries, but in most places, the evolution of the ecosystem is benefiting and will help sustain a more viable and longer-term startup environment.

To sum up, Asia's diverse culture and deep pool of regulations present a complex setting for startup founders. If they want to create groundbreaking businesses, they have to grasp the context in which they're operating. That means understanding the Asian landscape—its myriad of local cultures and its many layers of regulation. It's not enough to know just one side of this coin; founders must know both sides to build startups that can thrive in Asia. Some might think this is an enormous task, and it is—it's daunting for founders who are starting from scratch. But it can also be a competitive advantage for them if they put in the effort to achieve this seemingly Sisyphean task.

CHAPTER 3: BUSINESS MODEL ERRORS

In the kaleidoscopically changing world of Asian startups, the selection and implementation of business models are critical to dividing lines between success and failure. This chapter addresses some major strategic mistakes regarding business models that have doomed otherwise promising ventures throughout the region and, in doing so, provides a number of lessons for entrepreneurs, investors, and policymakers alike.

Business Model and Market Fit: Misalignments

Probably the most important mistake across failed Asian startups could be regarding business models not being well-oriented towards fulfilling the specific needs of target markets. This can be due to:

1. **Overestimating the Readiness of the Market**: This is probably one of the most common mistakes that happen because most startups have products or services well ahead of the needs or infrastructure of their target market.
    - *Example*: An Indian startup with an advanced AI-powered personal finance app found itself unable to get enough interest in a market where a large chunk of people are still transitioning from basic paper-based banking to digital banking.
2. **Local Competition Underestimation**: Some startups, especially those with foreign investors, have misunderstood the strength and

agility of local competitors, knowing inside the market and having established networks.
    - *Example*: The US-backed e-commerce platform in Southeast Asia lagged behind local players like Lazada and Shopee due to the fact that they knew more about local consumer behavior and logistics challenges.
3. **Misjudging the Cultural Nuances**: Most business models that work in one country in Asia end up complete failures in another because of silent yet striking cultural differences.
    - *Example*: While a dating app clicked in South Korea, the same had a very hard time penetrating Japan, where dating norms and social expectations remain considerably different.

To avoid such pitfalls, startups need to conduct intensive market research, participate in deep local partnerships, and be ready to alter their business models according to real-life feedback received from target markets.

Lack of Market Research and Analysis of Consumer Behavior

The lack of proper market research coupled with the lack of accurate analysis of consumer behavior - contributed to the failure of several startups in Asia. Some of the key factors that come into play here include:

1. **Being out of date or using irrelevant data**: Utilizing outdated market data automatically leads to misguided strategies in rapidly evolving Asian markets.
    - *Example*: A Chinese electric vehicle start-up planned production based on 2018 market data, not accounting for the explosive growth and shifting consumer preferences in the EV market between 2018 and 2021.
2. **Wrong Perception of Consumer Need**: More than a few startups slipped into projecting their perception upon the

consumers, rather than trying to understand what customers need and what exactly the pain points are.
    - *Example*: A Singapore-based health tech startup has come up with an advanced wearable device for elderly care, only to find that both elderly users and their caregivers favored solutions that are simpler and less intrusive.
3. **Lack of consideration for country-to-country and sometimes intra-country variations**: Too many pan-Asian strategies have bitten the dust because they have not accounted for the fact that basic consumer behavior may vary seriously across countries or even regions within countries.
    - *Example*: A food delivery app that took urban centers in Indonesia by storm found its match in the smaller cities, where habits related to eating out were different and digital adoption rates were much lower.

Quantitative and qualitative investment in local market research is therefore necessary on a continuous basis for any startup, through the participation of potential users and insight from various industry experts, to avoid such risks.

Overestimation of Demand and Resources

The supposition of inflated market demand and resource availability has been one of the major factors that have contributed to overexpansion for numerous Asian startups, which has resulted in quick cash burn and unsustainable operations.

1. **Miscalculating Market Size**: Several startups have based their business models on estimates of a larger total addressable market than what really existed.

- *Example*: A Malaysian Edtech startup offering English language tutorials had overestimated how many consumers would be willing to pay for premium online language courses. The result was less-than-expected revenue and eventual closure.
2. **Poor Estimate of CAC**: The cost of customer acquisition can be much higher than estimated in aggressive Asian markets.
    - *Example*: A Vietnamese e-wallet startup underestimated the required marketing spend it needed to fight with established players and depleted its funding before it was able to achieve a sustainable active user base.
3. **Operational Efficiency is Overestimated**: Therein lies the failure of some startups to account for complexities and inefficiencies that come with the supply chains and logistics networks across Asia.
    - *Example*: A Southeast Asian cross-border e-commerce platform was met with surprise delays and additional costs in both customs clearance and last-mile delivery, eroding its promised value proposition for customers.

These are problems that startups can mitigate by embracing more conservative financial modeling, factoring in significant buffers against contingencies, and placing efficiency and sustainability over aggressive scaling.

Adoption of Western Business Models Without Proper Localization

The second mistake that has continued to occur has been by both local and foreign-backed startups in Asia: the wholesale adoption of Western business models without proper localization.

1. **Neglecting Local Payment Preferences**: A number of e-commerce and FinTech startups have already gone bust because of not adapting to the local mode of payments and financial behavior.
    - *Example*: Digital wallet startup in Indonesia: The team started off with integration toward credit cards, which is not that popular among local consumers, who prefer bank transfers or even cash-based transaction settlements.
2. **Miscalculating Social Network Dynamics**: The usage and affinity towards social media in Asia are usually different from the Western markets.
    - *Example*: While an application based on social networking did well in the US, the same app failed to kick off in Japan and South Korea, where people use more anonymous and feature-heavy applications like Line and KakaoTalk.
3. **Negligence of Traditional Distribution Channels**: Many startups became overdependent on digital channels and underestimated the role of traditional retail and distribution networks that dominate many markets in Asia.
    - *Example*: A D2C beauty brand initially failed in India because it had a pure online play but later succeeded when it integrated with local beauty salons and retail stores.

This means that successful adaptation requires a deep understanding of the local market dynamics and a will and ability to fundamentally rethink business models for each target market.

Case Studies of Business Models Gone Wrong and Lessons Learned

To illustrate the above points, let us draw upon three case studies of Asian startups that failed owing to business model missteps:

1. **Honestbee (Singapore)**
    - *Business Model*: On-demand grocery delivery and online laundry services
    - *Key Issues*: Rapid expansion without sustainable unit economics, overestimation of market readiness across diverse Asian markets
    - *Lessons Learned*: Growth into profitability in core markets is principal before expansion while engaging in respect to country-specific strategies in every country

2. **Zilingo (Singapore/Thailand)**
    - *Business Model*: B2B platform of fashion supply chain
    - *Key Issues*: Pivot from B2C to B2B without ample market validation. Over-estimation of technology adoption rates by traditional industries
    - *Lessons Learned*: Importance of thorough market research before major pivots, challenges of disrupting traditional industries in Asia

3. **Ofo (China)**
    - *Business Model*: Dockless bike-sharing
    - *Key Issues*: Unsustainable unit economics, operational challenges, and competition were underestimated.
    - *Lessons Learned*: How important it is to have sustainable models in shared economy verticals, the risk of prioritizing growth over profitability.

These case studies, therefore, elaborated on the following key factors that contribute to success:

- Thorough, ongoing market research

- Adaptable business models can pivot based on market feedback
- Focus on unit economics and path to profitability
- Understanding of local cultural and business norms
- Realistic assessment of operational challenges in each market

These failures, discussed in this chapter, make it clear that creating successful startups in Asia's diverse and fast-changing markets is not an easy task. Though the region provides enormous opportunities, equally it produces unique challenges that need to be confronted with caution.

Successful Asian startups of the future will likely be those that:

1. Conduct extensive, ongoing market research
2. Develop adaptable business models that adjust to local market conditions
3. Favor sustainable unit economics over aggressive scaling
4. Be attuned to cultural nuance and local consumer behavior
5. Establish deep partnerships and knowledge networks

By following these guidelines—which represent lessons learned from the mistakes of their forerunners—the new cadre of Asian entrepreneurs will be better positioned to create more resilient businesses that are market-fit for long-term success in both local and global markets.

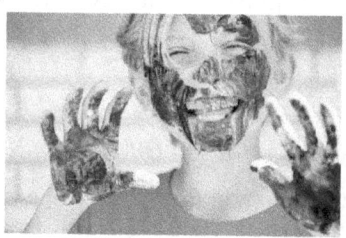

CHAPTER 4: FINANCIAL AND FUNDING MISMANAGEMENT

The dynamic face of Asian startups rests fairly on effective financial management and funding approaches. This chapter studies some common financial mistakes they made that brought promising regional ventures to their knees and summarized valuable lessons for entrepreneurs, investors, and financial strategists altogether.

Too Dependent on Venture Capital and Incorrect Allocation of Funds

Although venture capital drowned Asian markets with opportunities, they are also full of challenges for startups. Indeed, access to venture capital is important for growth, but excessive dependence on VC funding and misappropriation of such funds have caused some serious issues:

1. Asian startups tend to pay too much attention to vanity metrics—big numbers that look good on paper and please investors but are not growth metrics of healthy, sustainable businesses. Most of the time, they are under pressure from investors to "scale or die," which is, quite frankly, the narrative in a lot of Asian tech ecosystems. In this environment, ride-hailing companies in Southeast Asia have taken the bait and subsidized rides like crazy to gain market share, burning through millions in VC funding along the way.

2. Poor Focus on Essential Business Development: Some startups sink a huge amount of funding into activities that are unrelated to their core business and completely miss the development of the essential value proposition. Take, for instance, a Chinese AI startup that concentrated on blockchain technology and cryptocurrency projects not relevant to AI and used its competitive advantage in AI to fund what became a diversion.
3. Poor financial planning and forecasting: The vast majority of startups simply do not make stringent financial models and forecasts, which results in making poor decisions and allocating resources in the wrong direction. Case in point: An Indian e-commerce startup greatly overestimated its revenue and gross margin growth, while it seriously underestimated its operational costs; the result was a cash crunch when it hit the market.

Mitigation Strategies:

- Clearly spell out the roadmap of funding based on milestones
- Invest in key business activities
- Create strong financial planning and forecasting systems

Perils of "Growth at All Costs" Mentality

So far, the "growth at all costs" mentality, driven by the easy availability of VC funding and pressure to reach unicorn status, has led many Asian startups in a race for expansion at all costs while forgoing the building of sustainable business models.

1. **Unsustainable Strategies of Customer Acquisition:** Most startups have used high discounting and subsidies in customer acquisition, without clarity on customer retention or monetization strategy. *Example: An Indonesia-based food delivery startup gave huge discounts to attract users. Once the promotions were*

over, the platform was unable to hold on to the users, leading to a high churn of customers and surmounting losses.
2. **Premature Scaling:** Scaling into new markets or product lines too fast before nailing the core business has brought down many venture capital-backed startups. *Example: A Singapore-based co-working space provider rapidly expanded across Southeast Asia, only to face significant losses when occupancy rates failed to meet projections.*
3. **Neglecting Unit Economics:** In their pursuits of growth, several startups have forgotten the focus on unit economics improvement which has resulted in unsustainable business models. *Example: A last-mile delivery startup in India focused on growing its area of operations without correcting the basic unprofitability of every delivery, thereby forcing the shutdown of the company.*

To avoid such pitfalls, startups should:
- Focus on sustainable growth metrics and customer retention
- Prioritize unit economics improvement before scaling
- Elaborate on specific criteria for market entry and new product introduction

Cash Flow Crises and Burn Rate Management

One of the major causes of failure among Asian startups has been poor management of cash flow and burn rate. Specific causes include:
1. Runway Requirements Are Often Underestimated: Many of the nascent companies that we have worked with—especially those in the fintech sector—have failed to account for the runway they would need in the event of a funding delay or downturn. One Malaysian fintech company we worked with ran out of cash despite having the basic framework of a potential marketable product and waiting (in a very calm investor environment) for the next round of funding.

2. Inadequate Monitoring of Burn Rate: Not keeping the burn rate low and not keeping an eye on the rate will spell disaster for a young company. The company will run out of money far too quickly and with far too few changes in direction (if any) to respond to market signals. Example: A U.S.-Korean gaming startup lost funding faster than it could see a return on investment —before the finished game could hit the market and prove profitable.
3. Absence of Financial Discipline: When initial funding is sufficient, some startups do not install necessary financial controls or accountability mechanisms. For example, a Chinese Edtech startup discovered that its executives were spending excessively and without authorization, thus depleting its cash reserves and risking bankruptcy.

Cash flow management is needed to improve

- Detailed cash flow projections on a regular basis
- Robust financial monitoring and control system
- Contingency plans for funding delays or any possible market downturn

Smooth Funding Rounds: All Challenges

Many startups in Asia are seriously facing the challenge of overcoming the complexities regarding funding rounds.

1. Overestimation and Down Rounds: If expected growth is not met in later financing rounds, high early-round valuations can create problems. For example, a speculative Japanese AI startup managed to secure funding at a high valuation. After it staggered and failed to deliver on its promises, that speculative valuation was used against it in a much lower "down round," leading to founder dilution and loss of key investor confidence.

2. Misalignment with Investor Expectations: When a company's aims and objectives aren't consistent with those of its investors, friction can result that complicates the company's ability to raise funds in successive rounds. For example, an agritech startup in Indonesia is focused on making a long-term impact in the metrics that it sees as crucial. Its VC investors, however, are much more concerned with obvious and immediate signs of impact that would enable them to scale up their investment and achieve what they think of as a successful "exit."
3. Inadequate Due Diligence Preparation: A great many startups simply do not prepare well enough for the necessary due diligence that occurs before a funding round can happen. The result of this lack of preparation is frequently that the funding round does not happen, at least not on any reasonable timeline. One telling example: a promising Vietnamese e-commerce startup lost its Series B funding round opportunity because it could not supply clear, consistent, and timely financial information or necessary documentation for the would-be lead investor to look at during the crucial due diligence period.

Funding rounds could be better managed by:

- Keeping valuations in line with realistic business metrics in reality
- Business strategies and timelines being clearly communicated to investors
- Early implementation of strong systems for finance and operations

Failed Startup Cases due to Financial Mismanagement

With the given points above, we will look into three case studies of Asian startups and their only cause of going bust was mismanagement in financials.

1. Jawbone - Hong Kong/USA
    - Issue: The company's business model never allowed it to be self-sufficient, resulting in continued reliance on venture capital and no clear path toward profitability.
    - Resolution: This business model needs to change, and it needs to couple that change with some innovation in its product lines.
2. Homestay - Singapore
    - Issue: It's burning cash at an alarming rate, and it doesn't have a handle on unit economics yet. It also doesn't have a clear growth strategy to get it to profitability within a reasonable time frame.
    - Resolution: This company needs to do some serious soul-searching. Some might say it needs to look for a more realistic path to either sustainability or clear, sellable growth.
3. Aihuishou - China
    - Issue: It's all well and good to be a rapidly expanding tech company in China that operates in a space like e-commerce, but how do you manage cash flow during times of high growth?
    - Resolution: This company needs to get a handle on unit economics and ensure proper cash flow to keep the lights on and the business functional during the good times and the bad.

Optimal Financial Planning, Risk Management, and Capital Allocation

Drawing on this comparative best practice from the successes and failures within the Asian start-up ecosystem, the following may be identified: best practices in financial management include:

1. Comprehensive Financial Planning and Reporting. Create intricate, multi-scenario financial models. Regularly refresh projections to ensure they align with actual results. Put in place clear systems and processes for financial reporting, down to the level of individual project companies, that all constituents—financiers, managers, and others—can understand.
2. Concentrate on Sustainable Unit Economics. Achieve sustainable unit economics before scaling. Analyze and optimize CAC and LTV regularly.
3. Harmonize Expansion with Earnings. Establish key milestones for both expansion and earnings performance. Direct team incentives toward growth and financial health metrics.
4. Broaden Your Funding Base. Seek out alternatives to venture capital. Explore strategic partnerships, grants, and debt financing, and nurture relationships with all of the above. If you can accomplish that, then you can count on much more flexibility in your funding path.
5. Robust Corporate Governance. Assemble a capable board of directors whose members bring a variety of relevant experiences to the table. Put in place clear-cut policies governing financial decision-making and a system of checks and balances to maintain control.
6. Establish a Financially Responsible Culture. Be open about the company's financial condition. Teach your employees about the company's key financial indicators and the company's overall financial health and why those things matter.
7. Prepare for Market Ups and Downs. Retain enough cash reserves so that the business can weather a temporary slowdown without panicking. Don't just imagine one possible future; map out several and plan how you'll respond to each.

The financial foundation of such an Asian startup will thus get much stronger and will be more capable of withstanding any challenge that comes along with sudden growth or fluctuation in market conditions by following these best practices.

Put differently, while Asian startups are full of tremendous opportunities, they indeed come with some special kind of financial challenges. It is from the failures of the past that this next wave of Asian entrepreneurs will be able to learn and set up strong financial management practices aimed at building more sustainable and financially sound businesses for long-term success across the region and the globe.

CHAPTER 5: LEADERSHIP AND TEAM MISPLAYS

Effective leadership and team dynamics are the criterion factors that make an enterprise work seamlessly. Asian startups are no exception to this, and with startups being thrust headlong into a highly competitive setting in which every minute counts, these are only just a few things that hang in the balance. This chapter digs deep into the specific challenges revolving around effective leadership and team dynamics in Asian startups and how these challenges have dictated the failure of startups all over the continent.

Impact of Hierarchical Leadership on Innovation and Decision-Making

Indeed, many Asian cultures traditionally have placed huge emphasis on hierarchical structuring, and this can have an enormous consequence on the patterns of leadership and decision-making within startups.

Snuffing out innovation:

It will be immensely negative if hierarchical leadership suppresses the innovative ideas of juniors, misses opportunities, and results in stagnation.
Example: A highly promising South Korean fintech startup utterly failed to flex towards changing market conditions due to its inability to take up the input of junior members of the group, who could be more sensitive to rising trends.

Slow Decision-Making Processes:

Too much control through top-down decision-making could result in slowing down the speed at which decisions are made and losing market opportunities.
Example: An e-commerce startup in Singapore lost considerable market share to competitors who could make quicker decisions since every strategic decision needed to be approved by the founder himself, which often clogged up the decision-making process.

Risk Aversion:

In hierarchical organization systems, leaders might get alienated from grassroots realities-a factor contributing to overcautious decision-making.
Example: A Japanese AI startup lost out on a very lucrative partnership because midlevel managers refused to go to top leadership with a very risky yet potentially game-changing proposition.

To overcome these challenges, Asian startups should not do the following:

- **LESS** Flattened organizational structures
- **MORE** Open lines of communication at all levels
- **ESTABLISH** A formal process for submitting ideas and procedures to evaluate
- **EMPOWER** Middle management to make decisions

Building Cohesive Teams in Diverse Cultural Contexts

The rich cultural diversity in the Asia region, therefore, creates special challenges and opportunities in building teams for startups.

Cultural Misunderstandings

The lack of comprehension with regard to communication styles, work habits, and culture may lead to misunderstanding and, consequently, friction in the team.

Example: An Indian startup recently expanded to Southeast Asia and faced internal conflict because misaligned expectations on working hours and communication style between its Indian and Indonesian staff members caused prevailing tension.

Language Barriers

One particular challenge this poses for a multinational team is lower proficiency in the English language, quite capable of obstructing active communication and sharing of knowledge.

Example: A Chinese startup's expansion into Japan was stonewalled due to the communication gaps between Chinese-speaking leadership and Japanese-speaking local staff, misaligned objectives, and poor market penetration.

Diversity as Strength

Cultural diversity is an asset when positively applied and brings many points of view and new ideas.

Example: This Malaysian startup went all over Southeast Asia because it used its multi-cultural team to develop products that took advantage of other markets and easily gave the less diversified competition a run for its money.

Strategies for Cohesive Multicultural Teams

- Cultural Sensitivity Training
- Clear Communication Protocols
- Cross-Cultural Team-Bonding Opportunities
- Inclusive, Strong Company Culture that Blurs Across National Boundaries

Talent Acquisition and Retention Challenges in Competition with MNCs

More often than not, Asian startups face challenges in attracting and retaining elite talent due to the presence of well-established MNCs.

Limited Talent Pool

This is the case in most Asian markets, where demand for skilled professionals in the tech and other high-growth sectors often surpasses supply.

Example: A Vietnamese edtech startup had to scale its engineering team, owing to the limited experienced developers who were attracted to better-paying MNC roles.

Compensation Disparities

Startups typically cannot match salaries and benefit packages that the MNCs can offer; thus, it is hard to attract experienced professionals.

Example: A Taiwan hardware startup lost some of its key engineers to major tech firms; this delayed product development and missed critical market windows.

Perceived Job Security

In many cultures in Asia, perceived job security is an issue, and working for a startup firm may be viewed as quite a riskier career choice.

Example: It was the case with one of the Indonesian promising fintech startups: high turnover rates because employees hankered for more "stable" jobs in banks and established financial institutions to hold up the growth of a company.

Talent Acquisition and Retention Strategies

- Highlight equity, learning opportunities, and work-life balance as part of non-monetary benefits
- Employer branding that really emphasizes what is so special and different about working in a startup environment
- Mentoring and well-defined career pathways
- Strong company culture promotes loyalty and commitment towards long-term service.

Cultural Conflict and Team Performance

As startups expand into Asian markets or take in foreign talent, cultural clashes can be dramatically evident in team performance.

Differences in Management Style

The divergent expectations from management styles in different cultures can cause friction and lost productivity.

Example: A Singapore-based startup faltered in its move into Japan, as the direct communication of its Singaporean leadership conflicted with the indirect style that favored consensus, preferred by Japanese members of the team.

Work-Life Balance Expectations

Different cultural norms regarding proper work hours versus private life have contributed to friction within teams and burnout.

Example: A Korean startup that chose to expand into Southeast Asia faced some miscommunication when expectations to put in long work hours by Korean team members clashed with emphasis from local employees on work-life balance, leading to resentment and lowering productivity.

Decision-making processes

The differences among cultures about how decisions are made and how they are communicated create misunderstandings and delays.

Example: A Chinese startup working with an Indian team felt that the latter's consensus-based approach to decision-making resulted in decisions being very slow. The Chinese team members were frustrated because of this.

Strategies that help mitigate cultural clashes include:

- Cross-cultural training for all members
- Clear, culturally sensitive communication and decision-making protocols
- Open dialogue on cultural differences and expectations
- Hybrid culture that brings in pieces from different cultural backgrounds

Case of Leadership Failures and Disintegration of Teams

The above-mentioned points are more elaborated by taking the case studies of three Asian startups that failed due mainly to issues in leadership and team dynamics:

1. **Honestbee (Singapore)**
    - Problem: Lack of transparent leadership and Poor management of teams during high-growth scaling
    - Lessons: How open communication and cohesion at all levels of teams are to be preserved during growth phases
2. **Zefo (India)**
    - Problem: Failed to retain key talent in a competitive market
    - Lesson: The importance of competent retention policies and attractive employee value propositions

3. **Youche (China)**
    - Problem: Culture shock and breakdown in communications after an international scale
    - Lesson: Cultural fit and established channels for communication are critical to cross-border operations.

Leadership Strategies and Team Building to Bootstrap Innovation

From a mix of those who succeeded and those who failed within the Asian startup ecosystem, we will be able to highlight a few of the key strategies for leadership and team management:

1. **Make Adaptive Leadership Styles:**
    - Be adaptable with the leadership approach in view of the diverse cultural contexts.
    - Clearly give direction but at the same time empower the team.
2. **Embed a Culture of Innovation:**
    - Include ways of generating and evaluating ideas at every level.
    - Allow an enabling environment where experimentation is safe and allows for learning from failures.
3. **Emphasize Diversity and Inclusion:**
    - Seek to diversify actively by recruitment and decision-making.
    - Make all voices genuinely heard and valued through inclusion initiatives.
4. **Invest in Continuous Learning and Development:**
    - Provide regular training and development opportunities to all team members.

- Encourage knowledge sharing and cross-functional learning.

5. **Lay Down Clear Communication Protocols:**
   - Devise ways of effective communication at various cultural dimensions.
   - Leverage technology tools to assure smooth communication even in remote and distributed teams.

6. **Foster Strong Company Culture:**
   - Create and always reinforce the core values that are synonymous with every culture.
   - Organize team bonding and cultural exchange activities.

7. **Establish Effective Conflict Resolution Mechanisms:**
   - Develop explicit conflict resolution processes
   - Conflict resolution techniques-cross-cultural-training of leaders

8. **Balance Local and Global Perspectives:**
   - Combine local market knowledge with best global practices
   - Globally oriented leadership team with a thorough understanding of local markets

With such initiatives, Asian startups would be better positioned to build robust teams that are innovative and integrated-which can surmount complex challenges in the diverse markets of the region.

In summary, while the Asian startup ecosystem is a peculiarly tough environment for leadership and team building, tremendous opportunities are still there to be seized by those who know their way around such complexity. The next generation of Asian entrepreneurs can build businesses that are more sustainable, innovative, and globally competitive by learning from past failures and setting in motion appropriate leadership and team-building practices.

The success of Asian startups will in coming years depend greatly on whether they can instill in themselves leadership that is culturally sensitive yet globally-minded, or build diverse, cohesive teams that would allow them to thrive in the fast-paced multicultural environment of Asian and global markets.

CHAPTER 6: MARKET ENTRY AND EXPANSION BLUNDERS

Market entry and expansion are the two most critical yet most difficult tasks for a startup in dynamically different Asian markets. The authors discuss common mistakes made while developing a strategy for market entry; scaling across fragmented markets of Asia; scaling prematurely before consolidating existing markets; and overexpansion as a result of pressure to perform, emanating from funding.

Common Mistakes in Market Entry Strategies

Most Asian startups tend to go awry when trying to enter new markets for the following reasons, among others:

1. Lack of Market Research: Most startups do very little proper market research. If the market research is poorly conducted, one's product is not in line with what is needed, and marketing strategies will not work.

Example: An Indian food delivery startup that succeeded in its home market of India attempted to expand into Japan without doing proper homework on how people order food from restaurants in the country and what competition already existed. An app-based model that worked seamlessly in India's mobile-first market found itself at a loss in Japan, where most of its older demographics still relied more on phone ordering than app-based services.

2. Underestimating Cultural Differences Not taking the time to localize products and services and also communications strategies to local culture condemns the company to poor uptake.

Example: A Chinese social network went to Indonesia without considering the high conservatism of Indonesians in their social way of life. Features that had gained popularity in China, such as live streaming, now received regulatory challenges and backlash from its users in Indonesia.

3. Poor Localization The translation of an app or website is often not enough; true localization means adaptation to local tastes, ways of paying, and user interface.

Example: A Singapore-based e-commerce platform that expanded into Vietnam did not adapt to include popular local payment options such as cash on delivery and mobile wallet payments, thus shrinking the potential user base significantly.

4. Lack of Attention to Regulatory Compliance The inability to explore twists and turns in usually non-transparent regulatory environments could result in legal issues and operational roadblocks.

Example: A South Korean fintech startup expanded its operation into Thailand when it did not understand the fundamental legal grounds of the finance and economy of that country. They had to spend so much time and a lot of expenses in getting the license required to operate, thus giving their local competitors a chance to share in the market.

To limit these risks, startups follow these advises:

1. invest in professional, objective market research and local partnerships;

2. develop flexible business models adaptable to different cultural contexts;
3. pay more attention to deep localization of products and services;
4. contact local legal and regulatory experts in the early stage of expansion.

Challenges of Scaling Operations Across Fragmented Asian Markets

The diversity and fragmentation in Asian markets indeed introduce some very unique scaling challenges:

1. Diverse Consumer Preferences There is huge diversity in consumer preferences across Asian countries; sometimes this even occurs across regions within the same country.

Example: A Malaysian halal food delivery platform struggled to find similar success when expanding to non-Muslim majority countries like Thailand and Vietnam, where demand for halal food was limited to a niche market.

2. That means different levels of Internet penetration, smartphone adoption, and payment ecosystems all suggest a different tech stack and adaptable business models.

Example: An Indian Ed-tech startup had taken a mobile-first approach to rural Indonesia but needed to invest in offline learning solutions owing to very low smartphone penetration and internet connectivity.

3. Complex Supply Chain and Logistics Each market may require unique supply chain and logistics solutions, adding complexity and cost to expansion efforts.

Example: A Singapore-based e-commerce startup underestimated the logistical challenges of operating in Indonesia's archipelago and thus experienced delayed deliveries and dissatisfaction from customers.

4. Talent Acquisition and Management Forming local teams with the right mix of capabilities with cultural understanding is an often challenging task.

Example: While expanding to Vietnam, a Hong Kong-based AI startup found few qualified data scientists; they had to invest in extended training programs for local talent.

Strategies to Scale Effectively:

- Develop modular, adaptable business models and technology stacks
- Invest in strong local teams and partnerships in each market
- Prioritize markets based on strategic fit and readiness for your solution
- Build robust, flexible supply chain and logistics networks

Scaling Too Early and What It Leads To

This pressure to scale fast causes many startups to fall into the trap of scaling before they even have a solid foundation in place:

1. **Scaling Before Product-Market Fit** This can cause a waste of resources and a diffusion of focus when scaling up before having a clear product-market fit.

Example: A Thai health-tech startup, emboldened by initial success in Bangkok, jumped into rapid expansion across other Southeast Asian capitals without completing significant product refinement. The company extended its resources too far and thin, ultimately failing to meaningfully penetrate any market.

2. **Underestimating Operational Complexity** Rapid scaling has a tendency to unfurl operational inefficiencies and bottlenecks that were not visible on a smaller scale.

Example: Because an Indonesian last-mile delivery startup expanded operations to five major cities in just one year, it could not support burgeoning volumes with its centralized customer service model. As a result, unresolved customer complaints skyrocketed, seriously damaging its reputation.

3. **Neglecting Core Markets** This could make the company focus inordinate attention on the new markets and hence, it may cause them to forget their core market and lose their base.

Example: A very successful Vietnamese e-wallet provider charged headlong into a rapid expansion across three neighboring countries, away from its home market. Its local competitors caught up in Vietnam. This weakened this company's overall market position. It is essential to avoid early scaling.

The ways to avoid scaling blunders are as follows:

- The establishment of clear metrics associated with product-market fit can be considered before expansion

- Creation of operational processes which can be scaled and systems
- Expand only in core markets judiciously
- Create a solid financial foundation for long-term growth

Unsustainable Expansion due to Pressure from Investors

Investor expectations for phenomenal growth may force companies to adopt unsustainable expansion strategies. Such pressure arises in many ways, including the following:

1. Unrealistic Growth Expectations Exaggerated growth expectations from investors compel startups to enter unworkable markets or launch immature products.

Example: A Chinese smart home device manufacturer was forced by its investors to "globalize" and prematurely entered the U.S. market without sufficient product localization or brand building. The results were disappointing sales and negative reviews.

2. Misaligned Incentives When founder and investor incentives are not in a state of harmony, the consequences are short-term growth strategies at the cost of long-term sustainability.

Example: A Korean gaming startup, pressed by its investors to see breakneck growth in its user base, pursued aggressive means of acquiring users. The strategy proved to be unsustainable. This resulted in high churn rates and mounting losses.

3. Neglecting Profitability for Growth Overemphasis on user acquisition and revenue growth may result in an oversight of unit economics and the path to profitability.

Example: a Japanese meal-kit delivery startup, after investor pressure to capture market share, gave deep discounts to attract customers. This approach was unsustainable, with the company struggling to turn users into profitable, long-term customers.

Here are some strategies to help a firm manage investors and sustain growth:

- Clearly communicate realistic growth plans and potential challenges to investors
- Set metrics that balance growth with sustainability and profitability
- Find investors whose vision is in line with the company's long-term strategy
- Maintain a powerful board for balanced advisory counsel as well as for pushback when needed.

Case Studies of Unsuccessful Market Entry and Expansion

Let me elaborate on three such case studies of Asian startups that have failed in market entry or expansion:

1. Uber in China- Problem: Failure to anticipate local competition and regulation challenges; What to learn: How to adapt solutions for the fitment of the local market, and how to achieve good relations with the government
2. Foodpanda in Indonesia- Issue: Speedy expansion with lack of proper operational infrastructure; Lesson: Strong operational systems combined with local partnerships in scaling up complex markets
3. Rocket Internet's Ventures in Southeast Asia - Problem: Implementing a one-size-fits-all model across multivariate

markets; Lesson: The essential approach toward localization and how to understand subtle market differences

Scaling Up Sustainability and Successful Market Entry Strategies for Gradual Growth

Drawing from the successes and failures in the Asian startup ecosystem, there are a number of key strategies that point toward successful market entry and expansion:

1. Conduct Thorough Market Research • Perform deep market research on the ground before entry • Continuously collect and analyze market data to inform strategy
2. Prioritize Localization • Adapt products, services, and business models to local preferences and norms • Build local teams with strong market knowledge
3. Develop Flexible, Modular Business Models. Design flexible business models that can be easily replicated in other markets. Development of technology stacks able to support easy localization and scaling.
4. Emphasis on Sustainable Unit Economics or Focus on positive unit economics before aggressive scaling. Embed distinct metrics to measure sustainability and profitability.
5. Strong Local Partnerships. Engage with local partners in understanding and navigating regulatory and cultural landscapes. Leverage partnerships for market know-how and operational support.
6. Phased Expansion Strategies Develop overt criteria to prioritize markets and timing of entry Consider staged rollouts in order to prove out strategies before scaling
7. Focus on Core Markets and balance growth with further investment in core markets. Leverage insights from core markets to guide expansions

8. Set Investor Expectations Properly Present realistic growth plans to investors Seek out investors whose visions are in line with sustainable long-term growth strategies

These strategies, if implemented, would raise the probability of a successful market entry and further sustainable expansion of Asian startups. It's all about balancing ambition and prudence, growth and sustainability, global vision and local execution.

In their diversity and fragmentation, Asian markets are thus carrying as many opportunities as challenges for startup scale. The next generation of Asian entrepreneurs will be able to create truly pan-Asian or global businesses that are innovative and sustainable if they learn something from past failures and put in robust, adaptive strategies.

CHAPTER 7: PRODUCT DEVELOPMENT AND INNOVATION FAULTS

In the ever-changing landscape of Asian entrepreneurship, success versus failure widely depends on product development and innovation. This chapter reviews in great detail specific challenges that Asian startups face in terms of product development and innovation—from walking a tightrope between innovation and imitation, through the adoption of emergent technologies, to the borders of sustained innovation in the region.

Balancing Innovation and Imitation ("Fast-Follower" Strategy)

Most Asian startups actually walk a tightrope, balancing innovation in product development with the so-called "fast-follower" approach, rapidly replicating successful business models from other markets.

Benefits of the Fast-Follower Approach

1. **Lower Risk**: By adopting proven business models, startups can minimize some of the risks associated with a concept that is completely new.

Example: Grab in Southeast Asia took the model of ride-hailing pioneered by Uber and adapted it to the local market, turning itself into the regional leader almost overnight.

2. **Market Education**: Fast-followers can benefit from first movers' market education efforts. This decreases customer acquisition costs.

Example: Tokopedia, an Indonesian e-commerce platform, used the growing familiarity of online shopping created by earlier entrants to scale its business rapidly.

Pitfalls of Over-Reliance on Imitation

1. **Emphasize Non-distinction**: If one is merely to copy the existing models with little localization or enhancement, one invites commoditization, a.k.a. price wars.

Example: Proliferation of the indistinctive food delivery applications in major Asian cities led to an unsustainable price war and, finally, consolidation.

2. **Missed Opportunities for True Innovation**: Overdrive on Imitation sends startups into a trip where they fail to recognize native, uniquely local problems needing innovative solutions.

Example: A Singapore-based startup lost an opportunity to solve the peculiar challenges of Southeast Asian last-mile logistics because it moved too closely in step with Western e-commerce models.

Strategies for Effective Balance

1. **Local Adaptation**: Successfully adapting global models to meet local market needs and preferences.

Examples: Indian fintech startup Paytm adapted the concept of a mobile wallet for local conditions, integrating with small merchants and emphasizing QR code-based payments to suit the local market.

2. **Incremental Innovation**: Improve existing models with market-specific features and enhancements.

Example: Chinese super-app WeChat started as a messaging platform but innovated by integrating an array of services tailored to Chinese consumers' needs.

3. **Local Gaps**: Solve unique local problems that global models may fail to address.

Example: Indonesian startup Go-Jek realized the need for motorcycle ride-hailing through Jakarta's jammed thoroughfares, offering a category of service in its own right.

Technology Adoption and Leveraging of Emerging Technologies

The adoption and deployment of emerging technologies like AI, blockchain, and IoT take place in the Asian region either at the forefront or very early in the life cycle but this process also presents challenges.

Emerging Technologies Present Opportunities

1. **Artificial Intelligence (AI)**: Enormous innovation opportunities lie in this space across different industries.

Example: SenseTime, a Chinese AI company, used to be among the leading companies in facial recognition technology in the world, besides finding its takers in the realms of finance, security, and smart city projects.

2. **Blockchain**: This technology found fertile ground in Asia—from within both the fintech context and supply chain management.

Example: South Korean startup Blocko developed a blockchain-based digital certificate issuance service and subsequently had its solution adopted by major corporations and government agencies.
3. **Internet of Things**: IoT applications become one of the fastest-growing technologies of late, with ever-increasing usage, especially in manufacturing and smart cities.

Xiaomi in China evolved a successful ecosystem involving smart home devices that used IoT to create an integrated suite of product offerings.

Challenges to the Adoption of Technology

1. **Skill Gap**: Most Asian markets have a lack of skilled professionals in deep technologies.
   - As an example, the limited pool of senior machine learning engineers in the local market made it tough for a Vietnamese AI startup to scale up.
2. **Regulatory Uncertainty**: Most of the deep technologies exist in regulatory gray areas and hence come with risks to the startups.
   - Example: There were sudden attacks on cryptocurrency exchanges through regulations in several Asian countries, forcing many of them to shut down or relocate.
3. **Integration with Legacy Systems**: Most sectors are far behind in integrating the latest technology with their obsolete systems.
   - Example: A Japanese fintech startup had some problems integrating the blockchain-based solution with traditional banking systems, which made the adoption very slow.

Strategies for Successful Technology Adoption

1. **Investment in Training and Education**: The local talent in emerging technologies needs to be perked up with programs.

2. **Regulatory Engagement**: Engage proactively with regulators to influence favorable policies in relation to emerging technologies.
3. **Phased Implementation**: Technology implementation should be staged. It is better to start off with pilots and scale up based on the outcome.

Product Failures and Reasons Behind It

Product failures form a part and parcel of the struggle uphill that startups embark on, yet a peep into some common pitfalls helps in bringing down risks.

Common Causes of Product Failures

1. **Insufficient Product-Market Fit**: Products developed without adequate knowledge or understanding of market needs or user preferences.

Example: A Singapore startup created a too-sophisticated high-tech smart home system, too overpriced for the mass market, with the result of poor adoption.

2. **Poor User Experience**: Failure to maintain user experience as one of the key pillars in product or service design.

Example: An education technology platform from India, which boasted better content, couldn't mark its presence due to a faulty and unintuitive user interface.

3. **Poor Quality Control**: Introducing a poorly tested product into the market in a rush without proper quality checks.

Example: A Chinese smartphone company suffered badly when its flagship product was found to have major hardware problems just after its launch.

4. **Conflict with Local Culture**: Inability to adapt the product to local culture and tastes.

Example: A social network originating from Korea failed in Japan due to its features conflicting with the local expectations of privacy.

Product Failure Reduction Strategies

1. **Intensive User Testing**: Extensive user testing throughout the product development cycle.
2. **Iterative Development**: Using agile approaches in order to facilitate quick iterations based on user feedback.
3. **Cultural Sensitivity**: Avail local expertise and proper market research for cultural congruence.
4. **Quality Assurance**: Invest seriously in sound quality control processes, especially for hardware products.

Technological Lag and Innovation Barriers

While most Asian startups represent the bleeding edge of technology, there are a lot of innovation barriers that several of them have to put up with.

Causes of Technological Lag

1. **Bottleneck of R&D Investment**: Most Asian countries are still far behind in R&D investment accounting for the share of GDP.

Example: Despite its large tech sector, India's R&D spending remains below 1% of GDP, compared to over 2% in China and 3% in Japan.

2. **Brain Drain**: The topmost talent that Western tech hubs take away is one issue that slows down the pace of innovation in some Asian markets.

Example: Silicon Valley companies often recruit most of the top AI researchers from China and India, therefore creating a gap in home talent.

3. **IP Protection**: Poor IP protection in developing markets deters investment in truly breakthrough innovations.

Example: More than a few hardware startups in Southeast Asia would avoid local manufacturing for fear of IP theft, slowing down product development cycles.

Strategies to Overcome Innovation Barriers

1. **Government-Private Partnerships**: Scale government programs that increase R&D funding and support.
2. **Develop Appealing Work Environments**: Competitive compensation packages and challenging work environments will also retain the best talent.
3. **Invest in IP Protection**: Develop robust IP strategies and leverage international patents where necessary.

Case Studies of Innovation Failures

To illustrate these points, let's look at three case studies of Asian startups that have failed because of product development and innovation issues:

1. **Xiaomi's Mi Ecosystem**

Issue: Aggressive expansion into too many product categories with compromises on quality standards

Lesson: Focused innovation and strong quality control are extremely important

2. **Ofo's Bike-Sharing Platform**

Issue: Innovation stuck to the basic model. Operational challenges were not resolved.

Lesson shared: How sharing economy models continuously require innovation and operational excellence.

3. **Snapdeal's Marketplace Pivot**

Issue: Misjudging market trends. Inability to differentiate offerings within an increasingly crowded e-commerce sector.

Lesson shared: Need for keeping focus on core competencies during innovation

Best Practices to Ensure Product Development Success and Continuous Innovation

Drawing from the successes and failures in the Asian startup ecosystem, here are a few best practices that seem to emerge in the area of product development and innovation:

1. **User-Centric Design**: Give top priority to user needs and preferences right from conceptualization.
2. **Rapid Prototyping and Iteration**: Employ agile methodologies for fast testing and refining of product ideas.
3. **Localization**: Adapting global product concepts to market conditions and cultural fit of the local market.
4. **Balanced Innovation Strategy**: Balance "fast-follower" strategies with original innovation in solving selected local unique challenges.
5. **Strategic Technology Adaptation**: Be very selective while adopting emerging technologies, only at a realistic threshold of market needs and readiness for those technologies.
6. **Emphasized Quality Assurance**: In-depth double-check quality aspects, with particular emphasis on hardware products.
7. **Ongoing Market Research**: Monitor market changes and evolving customer needs.
8. **Collaborative Innovation**: Engage in partnerships with universities, research institutions, and other startups to further develop innovation capabilities.

9. **Talent Development**: Invest in training and retaining skilled professionals in key technological domains.
10. **IP Strategy**: Elaborate upon an all-inclusive intellectual property strategy to protect the innovations that would create long-term value.

By adhering to these best practices, Asian startups will be able to enhance product development processes and create cultures of continuous innovation needed to build sustainable businesses that can compete on a global level and address the unique challenges and opportunities provided by the diversity of Asia's markets.

In essence, product development and innovation within the Asian startup ecosystem pose both immense challenges and great opportunities for those who can get it right. By learning from past failures, leveraging local market insights, and implementing robust strategies for development and innovation, the next generation of Asian entrepreneurs enjoys great prospects with world-class products and services both regionally and globally

CHAPTER 8: REGULATORY COMPLIANCE CHALLENGES

The pace at which startups scale often makes them forget about regulatory compliance. These are young companies focused on rapid growth. Doing business in Asia, the Asian regulatory landscapes present an array of challenges. Legal frameworks all across the continent vary widely, sudden changes in policies do take place now and then while the markets are highly fragmented. That is particularly a huge undertaking for many Asian startups, ranging from the likes of FinTech and e-commerce to blockchain when local country regulations can be so very different not only between countries but even within the countries themselves. Non-compliance might result in costly fines, legal disputes, or even complete shutdowns. This chapter will review the trials in ensuring compliance, the risks of regulatory uncertainty, and strategies that companies can take to mitigate those risks. We will explain through case studies and practical examples how startups can turn a potentially adverse element into a strategic advantage.

Tackling Diverse and Rapidly Changing Legal Landscapes

One of the biggest challenges for startups operating across the region is indeed the diversity in legal systems and regulatory requirements. From data protection laws in Japan to restrictions on foreign ownership in Indonesia, each country applies a different set of rules that makes compliance complex for startups looking to expand regionally or internationally. Factors that vary across industries, including the regulatory environment: For example, fintech regulations on a payment system, cryptocurrencies, and digital banking can be very heterogeneous across countries. Take for instance Singapore, which is allowing progressive regulatory sandboxes for fintech innovations, to India, which allows the Reserve Bank to impose strict regulations on digital payments and foreign-owned fintech firms.

Case Study: Ride-hailing apps in Southeast Asia have to navigate the immensely labyrinthine ecosystem of local transportation laws, licensing requirements, and labor regulations that often vary dramatically within a single country. Many firms went through delays and protracted legal battles as local governments clamped restrictions on the ride-hailing services, significantly hampering growth and operations.

What really makes the regulatory environment complete is the pace of changes in policy. For a startup to keep up with new legislation and regulations, agility is required; however, few of them are ready for that, and hence non-compliance and other legal problems arise. In this respect, long-term success requires being informed about everything relevant and building relationships with local legal experts and regulators.

Impact of Sudden Changes in Regulations on Business Models

Sudden changes in regulations can have effects on even the very core of the business models, often making startups pivot. For instance, governments in Asia can introduce new regulations at very short notice. By the time the startups run around trying to comply, some of the resultant penalties can be very serious. This has been most documented in industries such as cryptocurrency, e-commerce, and the gig economy, where innovation outpaces regulation.

Cryptocurrency in China: The government of China has always been notoriously strict about cryptocurrency. In 2017, it issued a ban on initial coin offerings and literally shut down all crypto trading. Many startups were then forced to fold up operations or move their base to jurisdictions that were friendly towards them, such as Singapore and Japan.

Data Protection Regulations: The demand for the implementation of data protection regulations across Asia also influenced the business models. This includes the PDPA in Singapore and APPI in Japan, for which all these startups had to invest extensively in measures that helped protect data. For industries with a lot of data, like e-commerce, health care, and fintech, the list of regulations has gone up, making operations costlier.

For such instances, startups that quickly adapt to changes and ensure compliance could turn events in their favor. Failing to do so, on the other hand, may well place them under debilitating fines, loss of consumer trust, or even shutdowns.

Data Privacy and Security Concerns

Data privacy and security are rapidly becoming one of the most critical compliance issues that startups are dealing with in Asia, along with an increasing awareness of data protection among consumers. What really makes it even more challenging not just for startups but especially for those who need to handle cross-border data flow is that Asia has taken a pretty fragmented approach toward legislating laws on data privacy.

Case Study: GDPR and Asian Startups - Even though the General Data Protection Regulation of the EU centers on European companies, Asian startups operating or selling in Europe are equally liable under its stringent conditions. Non-compliance fines can reach enormous amounts, and many Asian startups were thus found off-guard by this regulation in 2018.

Local Regulations: Some countries, like South Korea, possess some of the most strict data privacy laws in the world. They include heavy fines in case of data breaches. Therefore, any startup based in such a nation must adhere to local laws, including PIPA in South Korea, that necessitate high standards of data protection and disclosure obligations.

Non-compliance with data protection regulations comes with heavy fines, reputational damage, and the consequences of losing customer confidence. This means that right from the very inception, a startup should be keen on ensuring data security by investing in compliance infrastructure such as hiring lawyers and developing transparent policies on handling data.

Compliance Failures Leading to Shutdowns and Legal Disputes

The risk of noncompliance can have severe consequences for a startup expensive litigation processes, significant monetary fines, and in the worst case, total shutdowns. This risk is particularly acute for those startups that do not have a good understanding of the local regulatory environment.

Case Study: OKCoin Fall OKCoin, once among the largest cryptocurrency exchanges in China, faced a major regulatory crackdown in the year 2017 when the government of China banned Cryptocurrency Trading. Once a glittering star in the crypto exchange industry, OKCoin was compelled to shut down all its operations in China. Given that it is really difficult to survive just by shifting headquarters, OKCoin suffered hugely in terms of market share and brand reputation.

Case Study: Food Delivery Platforms in India The Indian government imposed more strict food safety laws on food delivery startups, such as Zomato and Swiggy. Both of them passed an arduous test because these platforms had to take responsibility for the food safety standards of every restaurant on the network. Many restaurants disappeared overnight from the company lists, thereby affecting their market share and consumer trust.

For this reason, startups have to ensure that, right from the beginning, they develop a proactive compliance program that incorporates regulatory risk management within the larger business plans.

Best Practices to Ensure Compliance and Mitigate Regulatory Risks

Following are some best practices for ensuring compliance by a proactive approach to mitigate regulatory risks in any regulatory minefield in Asia:

- **Hire Legal Experts Early:** Perhaps one of the most important things a startup can do is get legal experts on board as early as possible. Legal experts are better positioned to help navigate through potential regulatory pitfalls and will be able to take steps to ensure that a company is compliant with regulations from day one.
- **Monitoring of Policy Changes:** This would involve monitoring the startups with respect to policy changes in the countries where they operate. This may be done by partnering the startups with local regulatory experts, who join industry associations to stay updated on impending changes, besides maintaining open lines of communication with regulators.
- **Develop Compliance-First Culture:** Compliance-first culture simply means developing alignment in teams from product development through marketing to meet regulatory requirements, hence reducing the probability of accidental non-compliance and creating a more robust and trustworthy brand.
- **Leverage Technology:** For the most part, the adoption of different RegTech solutions could be critically helpful for this class of startups in automating compliance processes and tracking changes in regulations.
- **Cross-border compliance:** Companies operating in various countries that are starting up should adhere to one approach to compliance. However, due to the fact that every country has its set of rules and norms, a comprehensive strategy could be drawn up for cross-border compliance. This would smoothen processes and minimize operational risks.

It is actually regulatory compliance that very often creates a difference between success and failure for startups in Asia. Although the diverse and fast-changing regulatory environment itself presents a real challenge, proactive startups can turn those very challenges into strategic advantages by embedding compliance-oriented operations from the very beginning and adopting a methodology toward continuous regulatory change. Past failures can be instructive for mitigating risks in protecting hard-earned brand reputation to thrive eventually in the fierce Asian market.

CHAPTER 9: MISSTEPS IN MARKETING AND SALES

In a highly competitive market like Asia, the success of any business depends on the adopted strategy for marketing, sales, and customer retention. At the same time, most startups sacrifice this very important aspect in their hurry to scale. The complexity and fragmentation in the markets of Asia further aggravate these challenges due to cultural diversity, market diversity, and rapidly changing consumer behaviors. Poor market fit, over-reliance on promotions or discounts for customer acquisition, and inefficient sales methods are just a few of the numerous reasons Asian startups have to face. Because of that fact, many startups have not been able to continue with long-term customer loyalty and, in the process, just fail.

This chapter highlights some of the most important challenges Asian startups face in their marketing, sales, and customer retention. We will be discussing the key reasons it is essential to understand local markets, and the dangers of prioritizing rapid growth at the expense of customer satisfaction, together with actionable insights and case studies on how to develop a sustainable customer-centric business.

Common Marketing and Sales Pitfalls in Asian Markets

Marketing in Asia is a whole different ball game due to the immense variety that exists across the continent. Understanding fragmented markets—from languages and cultures to economic disparities and internet penetration rates—is essential to a startup's success. However, many of them fall prey to a few commonplace pitfalls that prevent their growth:

- **Misaligned Marketing Strategies**: Most Asian startups simply use Western marketing strategies without adapting them to the local context. As an example, marketing campaigns that stress individualism will fall flat in collectivist cultures like China or Japan, where community and family values run deep. A one-size-fits-all approach rarely works in Asia.
- **Poor Localization**: To market effectively in Asia, deep localization is necessary; this goes beyond the simple translation of advertisements in the local language. Startups must also be aware of the local customs purchasing habits and regional peculiarities. E-commerce startups in Southeast Asia often underestimate how widespread a means of payment cash-on-delivery remains in countries like Vietnam and Indonesia.
- **Overreliance on Digital Channels**: While digital marketing is powerful in many parts of Asia, too often startups neglect the continued relevance of offline channels—particularly in the less developed markets. In rural areas of India and Indonesia, for instance, traditional media like television and radio still play an important role in reaching consumers.

Those not adapting their marketing strategies to local conditions are bound to turn potential customers off and give ground to more knowledgeable competitors in the regional landscape.

Customer Acquisition Challenges: The Limits of "Growth at All Costs"

While customer acquisition is a core element in the success of any startup, it has also been one of the main areas where many Asian startups fall for the "growth at all costs" mentality, basically an intense customer acquisition via heavy discounting and promotions. The result is often impressive in the short term but proves to be unsustainable over a longer period of time.

- **Case Study: E-commerce Price Wars**—In markets like India and Southeast Asia, a number of e-commerce startups, including Flipkart and Lazada, fought highly aggressive price wars by offering deep discounts as one avenue to secure new customers. This indeed drove customer acquisition at a fast rate, but profit margins were highly compressed to result in the creation of a customer franchise that seemed to be more loyal to discounts than to the brand in general.
- **High Customer Acquisition Costs**: This cost of acquiring customers through discounts, paid advertising, and promotions can increase really fast. In highly competitive industries such as food delivery and e-commerce, this becomes even more unbearable. Many startups have unsustainable costs of customer acquisition that they try to recover by value created through the lifetime of a customer.
- **Churn Rates and Brand Loyalty**: The startups that depend a lot on discounts for acquiring customers have high churn rates when the latter immediately move on to other competitors offering them better deals. This negates the chances of building brand loyalty in the long run and creates no competitive advantage.

This means a trade-off in rapid growth for sustainable customer acquisition because, in their strategies, startups should offer real value and build sustainable long-term relationships with all of their customers.

Customer Retention Failures and Consequences

Customer retention is just as important, if not even more so, than customer acquisition, yet it's the place where many Asian startups do not invest adequately. Poor retention could be terrible since the cost of acquiring a new customer generally runs five times higher than retaining an existing customer.

- **Zero Personalization**: In highly discerning markets like South Korea and Japan, startups that don't personalize suffer from poor customer retention. Customers would want the brand to understand their preference direction and thus provide them with customized products, services, or recommendations. Startups that settle for generic offerings simply miss an opportunity to engage with their customers on a closer level.

- **Customer Support**: Many startups in verticals like fintech and e-commerce tend to overlook the area of customer support due to which they end up losing their customers. In most Asian regions, especially, word of mouth or even online reviews can have a lasting effect on any brand's reputation.
- **Not considering the after-sales**: While a sale gets closed, a majority of the startups mark this transaction complete and forget to further engage with their customers. However, this may be part of post-sale engagement for effective long-term engagement and repeat business. A majority of the startups that don't invest in nurturing relationships later on witness their customers slowly drifting to rivals offering a comprehensive experience.

This means personal communication, high support of one's customers, and continuous involvement; all these features spell out the realistic retention strategies that have to be implemented in order to sustain growth and build up a loyal customer base.

Case Studies of Marketing, Sales, and Retention Failures

Failure analysis of past startups proves to be very useful in studying what mistakes are being made when developing marketing, sales, and customer retention strategies.

Case Study 1: The Failure of Honestbee in Southeast Asia

Honestbee, a grocery delivery startup from Singapore, expanded aggressively in Southeast Asia. However, aggressive discounting, poor localization, and over-reliance on customer acquisition without consideration for customer retention brought about its collapse. It burned its cash trying to onboard new users without nurturing a loyal customer base. At the end, it declared bankruptcy in 2019.

Case Study 2: WeWork in Asia

The ambitious expansion of WeWork into Asia completely failed to understand local market dynamics. The co-working giant has been offering a standardized product from Tokyo to Jakarta, without a thought for decent adaptation to meet local needs. High prices alienated customers in price-sensitive markets, while its failure to offer value beyond office space limited customer retention.

Case Study 3: Snapdeal Lost Its Market Share

Snapdeal once held greater market shares in India's e-commerce but later over-concentrated on ensuring price discounts and rapid expansion, both eventually causing this company to lose its market shares to other companies like Flipkart and Amazon. Snapdeal couldn't retain its customers due to a lack of post-sale support and inconsistent product quality, which seriously led to its sharp decline.

These cases illustrate the need to balance acquisition with retention, tailor offerings for local markets, and focus on long-term customer relationships.

Best Practices for Marketing, Sales, and Customer Retention in Asia

Considering both the competition and diversity of the Asian markets, the mere adoption of a holistic and customer-centric approach to marketing, sales, and retention is the key to success. Here are some best practices:

- **Localization is Key**: Startups need to invest in a deep understanding of local markets, cultures, and consumer behaviors. This goes beyond the mere translation of languages into the localization of products, marketing messages, and customer support to speak to the target audience.
- **Customer-centric Culture**: No strategy for any kind of startup can keep customers at the heart of its focus. This means pre-emptive customer service, swift action on customer feedback, and continuous product improvement based on user insights.
- **Stitching Data Together for Personalization**: At the heart of customer loyalty lies offering personalized experiences through customer data. Startups should make use of analytics to understand customer preferences, customize their marketing campaigns, and offer relevant recommendations.
- **Emphasize Long-term Relationships**: Startups that focus on long-term relationships with customers rather than just short-term gains will see more success. This includes post-sales engagement, loyalty programs, and community-driven marketing initiatives that develop a much stronger affinity with the brand.
- **Omni-Channel Marketing**: With such fragmented media consumption habits across Asia, adopting an omni-channel approach will serve startups best, where they integrate online and offline channels for effective audience reach.

In this way, marketing, sales, and customer retention would become the bedrock upon which startup success would be based. There are many challenges to navigate across this fascinating region because of its immense cultural diversity, highly fragmented markets, and fast-shifting consumer behaviors. Very few of them adapt their strategies to local contexts and prioritize short-term growth over long-term relationships, making it hard for these startups to survive. More so, startups will learn from the failures of others and then apply customer-centric, locally relevant, and data-driven approaches to create sustainable growth, and brand loyalty, and ultimately succeed in dynamic Asia.

CHAPTER 10: OPERATIONAL AND SUPPLY LAPSES

Operational and supply chain efficiency lies at the backbone of any startup's success, especially in the rapidly growing markets of Asia. However, a number of Asian startups insufficiently appreciate the complexities that arise when it comes to laying down and maintaining smooth operations and agile, resilient supply chains. The fragmented nature of the markets, inadequacies within the infrastructure, and regulatory hurdles often pose significant barriers to scaling. Furthermore, the startups that are not able to make resistant operational models are highly vulnerable to various sorts of disruptions, including the COVID-19 pandemic, natural disasters, and geopolitical tensions all factors that may seriously affect supply chains.

Besides scaling issues across fragmented markets, this chapter discusses the key operational and supply chain challenges faced by Asian startups. These discussions will range from topics on technological infrastructure to supply chain vulnerabilities. We shall be going through some case studies of such startups that faced operational inefficiencies and provided actionable insights and best practices for the building up of resilient and scalable operational frameworks.

Technology Infrastructure and Operational Issues

A key operational challenge faced by Asian startups in the region is the fact that the region has an insufficient technological infrastructure. While Asia has developed quite fast over the last couple of decades, some of its markets tend to lag in terms of digital infrastructure, which directly influences the capability of a startup to carry out seamless operations.

Inconsistent Internet and Communication Infrastructure

One of the major challenges in developing areas involves inconsistent internet connectivity, as noted in Southeast Asia and South Asia regions. As much as it affects inconsistent internet connectivity, it is also very far from having any digital tools. For example, such a weak infrastructure may disrupt the business operations of those startups that rely on cloud-based systems or digital supply chain management tools.

Case Study: E-commerce and Last-Mile Delivery in Indonesia

Indonesia has an archipelago structure that presents a number of logistical challenges. For example, different e-commerce startups, such as Tokopedia and Bukalapak, could not scale last-mile delivery services around the country since there was still a lack of transportation systems that connected rural and remote areas. This hurt their growth and level of customer satisfaction since delays in delivery and extra costs eroded customer satisfaction.

Technological Gaps in Manufacturing

There is inefficiency due to the use of obsolete technologies and a lack of automation in most manufacturing startups in countries like India and Vietnam. It Cuts the cycle of production, which is slower than it should be, and thus hampers meeting the market demand in time.

Startups should invest in technological solutions that can resolve the operational realities of the region they serve. A common example is the adoption of mobile-first solutions for overcoming infrastructural challenges or creating alternative logistic networks.

Supply Chain Vulnerabilities and Disruptions

Supply chain disruption is one of the key challenges that many startups from different parts of Asia face. Whether it's a natural disaster, geopolitical tensions, or a pandemic occurring somewhere worldwide, all these could give severe jolts to the supply chains and affect everything, from the procurement of raw materials to product delivery.

Supply Chain Impact from COVID-19

The COVID-19 pandemic brought abruptly into focus just how fragile global supply chains were. These startups relying on international suppliers for integral parts of their components found difficulty in delays and shortages whenever the lockdowns across the world hampered production and shipping. For instance, in industries like electronics and healthcare, the startups found extreme delays arising due to the closure of the manufacturing hubs in China and Southeast Asia.

Case Study: Semiconductor Shortages in Asia

During 2021, the global semiconductor shortage finally showed up; pan-industry startups, especially those in the automotive and electronic fields, were hit extremely hard. Any company not yet diversified in supply chain or strategic partnerships with suppliers faced critical delays to a product offering to the market and lost its grip on market share.

Natural Disasters

The Asia region is exposed to and/or prone to typhoons, earthquakes, and floods that could abruptly disrupt the supply chain. "These firms located in the areas prone to such calamities are supposed to make contingency plans and have multiple strategies to reduce their risks."

This also encompasses resilient supply chains that can absorb external shocks, diversify the network of suppliers, invest in local sourcing, and use the latest digital tools to constantly monitor and manage risks throughout supply chains.

Scaling Challenges in Fragmented Asian Markets

Scaling operations across Asia are very complex, given the economic, regulatory, and cultural diversities in the region. Those startups that scale up too quickly or without proper operational grounding often struggle with maintaining efficiency and profitability.

Fragmented Market

Today, Asia is not one big market but a collection of them. Each country throws up its operational challenge. For instance, expanding operations from Singapore to Indonesia means going through a completely different regulatory environment, consumer behavior, and logistical challenges. Startups that fail to adapt their operational strategy in each market face bottlenecks, which contribute to the slowing down of growth.

Case Study: Grab's Regional Expansion
As Grab expanded regionally across Southeast Asia, it needed to modify its operations model to fit the requirements of the various countries. For instance, Singapore-where credit card payments are very common. Grab had to introduce cash payment to accommodate the cash-based economies of the likes of Vietnam and Indonesia. The operation and logistical headaches arising from such disparate markets implied tremendous cost inflation.

Overexpansion and Inefficiency

Most startups, to satisfy their investors, start expansion prematurely before laying a strong operational infrastructure. This inevitably brings inefficiencies, increased costs, and operational bottlenecks that are hard to reverse.

The second thing is that scaling up successfully must be done in sequence, first establishing operational excellence in core markets before expanding into new ones. Another problem is that flexibility in operational models is something startups should strive to develop, operational models that would adapt to each particular market.

Case Studies of Operational Failures

Operational failure is probably the worst thing that could happen to any startup; it may come with huge financial losses, loss of reputation, and sometimes even cessation of business. The case studies from a failed startup provide an important lesson in building resilient and effective operations.

Case Study 1: Logistics Challenges of RedMart

RedMart, a Singapore-based online grocery delivery service, faced several operational issues in the initial days regarding the supply chain and last-mile delivery. The firm could not cope with demand and was always lagging behind in terms of delivery delay and 'out of stock' conditions. This operational inefficiency adversely hampered customer satisfaction, and this startup sold its operations to Lazada in the year 2016.

Case Study 2: AirAsia Logistics Subsidiary

The diversification into logistics carried out through its cargo and logistic subsidiary Teleport, had operational challenges in terms of experience in managing such a logistics network. As such, cargo handling and delivery services were not efficient, reflected in the below-par performance when competing with established regional logistics players.

Case Study 3: Rocket Internet's Foodpanda

Backed Foodpanda expanded aggressively across the continent of Asia. However, it later got burned by operational inefficiencies. In countries having really poor infrastructure like Bangladesh and Pakistan, the delivery of food was a logistical problem for the company. The high costs of delivery along with operational mismanagement have forced Foodpanda to scale down its operations in these regions.

These examples lead to one central point: setting good operational grounds before aggressive growth. When these startups do not look into operational efficiency, the scaling up often becomes insurmountable for them.

Best Practices for Operations Management and Building Resilient Supply Chains

Overcoming operational and supply chain challenges requires best practices that ensure the efficiency, scalability, and resiliency of the operations. Some strategies that will be of immense help include:

Scale Up Digital Transformation

Encourage the modern application of digital tools such as cloud-based supply chain management, AI-powered logistics optimization, and IoT sensors for operational insight by startups. Automation, real-time inventory control, and reduction of human errors with the use of digital tools contribute directly to operational efficiencies.

Diversify Supply Chains

Relying on one supplier or region may provide certain critical components, which are quite risky in times of disruptions. Therefore, the start-up should look towards diversification in their supply chains by sourcing from different suppliers across various regions. This will not only reduce the risk of supply shortages but also give more bargaining power on the negotiation table.

Agility in Operations

Agility is the key to operational success in the dynamic markets of Asia. Operations would be conducted following agile methodologies whereby a startup can move rapidly against changes in market conditions, regulatory environments, or even supply chain disruptions.

Focus on Local Sourcing

In markets with difficult infrastructures, sourcing materials or components locally can be very helpful for a startup. This ascertains a reduction in transport costs and helps mitigate the risk of disruptions within international supply chains.

Phased Scaling

The startup needs to scale its operations in phases. What is needed is to test the operational models in every new market before further expansion. This helps the startups realize various bottlenecks or inefficiencies that may arise well in advance.

Indeed, some of the biggest challenges Asian startups face are operational and supply chain-related. With highly fragmented markets, infrastructural gaps, and especially a vulnerability to disruptions, efficiency in operations and resilience in supply chains become key enablers of success. This would range from investment in digital tools to supply chain diversification and phased scaling. Following best practices allows for the establishment of operational building blocks that can pave the way for successful scaling. Indeed, learning from the failures of others can provide key lessons on how to avoid common operational pitfalls and achieve long-term growth in Asia's dynamic markets.

CHAPTER 11: CULTURAL AND SOCIAL MISMATCH

Culture and social dynamics are two of the key elements constitutive of any startup's success or failure in most parts of Asia because of the deeply ingrained attitude toward cultural values and relationship networks and their practice in business. Any startup that does not take these things into consideration is put at a disadvantage since it cannot work out the unseen rules of social conduct that control decisions across the region. Insight and integration with local cultures, acceptance of social expectations, and relationships based on mutual trust form the tripod upon which business success rests in Asia.

In this chapter, we shall discuss how cultural and social factors- such as guanxi, or relationship networks, the concept of "face," or reputation and honor, and the extremely hierarchical nature of most Asian societies affect startups. By examining case studies of those startups whose missteps in these areas cost them dearly, as well as those who successfully navigated the complex social landscapes, this chapter will provide an inside look at the role that culture plays in building resilient and successful businesses in Asia.

How to use Guanxi and relationship networks

The guanxi-or a system of social networks and influential relationships-plays a significant role in many Asian countries, most especially China, in personal and business life. It is often more critical to have good relations with key stakeholders, government officials, and business partners than it is to achieve the more traditional metrics of performance or financial success.

Trust

Because personal relationships often outrank formal contracts in many cultures, this is the social currency of business. That means a startup will be required to develop long-term relations with local partners, suppliers, and customers. If one does not have strong relationships, then securing partnerships or funding-or even regulatory approvals-may become tough.

Case Study: Uber's Struggles in China Certainly, one of the major causes that made Uber give up on China was just that it did not establish close relations with local regulators and businesses. Unlike its local rival, Didi, Uber failed to invest in building guanxi, which consequently led to regulatory hurdles and challenges in expanding its operations. Where Didi leveraged those relationships with key stakeholders for government support, it appears more confident about taking away market share.

Networking for Success

Most of the time, networking yields the key in Southeast Asia. Those startups that rigorously participate in the local business network, chambers of commerce, and other industry associations often acquire critical access to resources and insight that can facilitate their growth at a faster pace.

To those startups venturing into Asian markets, the development of proper guanxi is not a formality but an important strategic step toward gaining a competitive advantage.

The Concept of "Face" and Its Impact on Business Decisions

Face is a deep-seated social concept in most Asian societies, also referred to as MianZi in Chinese, Kao in Japanese, or naman in Korean. It involves reputation, honor, social standing, and how one interacts, decides on, and conducts business. In the world of business, this concept of face might influence negotiations, decision-making, and conflict resolution.

Avoiding Public Criticism

One of the touchy elements in maintaining face is to avoid public humiliation or criticism. In these hierarchical cultures, like China, Japan, and South Korea, to openly challenge or criticize a superior or a business partner will amount to a loss of face, and this might affect business relationships and dealings. This means that for startups, sensitive issues, disagreements, or performance feedback should be handled in privacy and with much care not to hurt feelings and cause loss of face.

Case Study: Toshiba's Corporate Crisis in Japan The 2015 accounting scandal at Toshiba points to the concept of face and its result in delaying the publication of financial misconduct. Senior executives wanted to avoid losing face by suppressing bad news. This habit results in a more significant reputational and financial crisis for the company.

Impact of Negotiations

Negotiations also take longer in societies where saving face is a central concept. Each party avoids confronting the other directly or making a move that may lead to one of the parties losing face. This understanding is important for startups, particularly during critical negotiations. Pressing too strongly for swift decisions can be counterproductive.

The unwritten rules defining social behavior are faced. Understanding the nuances of face will enable startups to do business with so much more cultural sensitivity, and that will go a long way toward helping them forge relationships that endure.

Hierarchical Societies and Leadership Challenges

In many respects, therefore, the Asian culture-be it in China, Japan, South Korea, or India-is intrinsically hierarchical; respect for authority and seniority is deeply inbuilt within both the social and organizational psyche. That brings an opportunity, as well as a challenge, for startups in regard to leadership, decision-making, and team dynamics.

Top-Down Decision Making

Decision-making in hierarchical societies is concentrated at higher levels of a company. The startups coming into these markets have to learn to live with the reality that decisions can hardly be made either in a fleet or collaboratively in big corporations or government institutions. Younger, junior employees in the ranks would be very hesitant to express contrary opinions, even when they know there might be some issues.

Case Study: Leadership Challenges of a Japanese Startup A Japanese technology industry startup finds its staff resisting the Western-trained CEO's efforts to encourage open debate and the sharing of ideas. The result is misunderstandings and delays in projects. Eventually, the CEO had to change his management style to fit local expectations about hierarchy and respect for authority.

Seniority Matters

A startup dealing with a government agency or a large corporation in South Korea or India should be ready to give respect to seniority and authority figures whenever negotiations and partnerships take center stage. One will experience misunderstandings or even the breakdown of business discussions whenever hierarchical norms are not observed.

As foreign startups or companies enter these markets, their leadership must attune to the hierarchical respect this basis of effective teamwork and partnerships in such markets requires.

Cross-Cultural Issues and How These Affect a Startup's Journey

Cultural misunderstandings can easily divert even the most promising startups that fail to maneuver the local market nuances effectively. Differences in the way people communicate, negotiate, and practice business etiquette tend to cause problems, mistakes, and fended feelings.

Communication Styles

Most Asian cultures are very indirect when it comes to communication, especially on sensitive topics. For example, a Japanese or Korean company would never say "no" to a request if they mean "no"; instead, they might provide a vague response. Those startups unfamiliar with such subtlety would sometimes end up incorrectly interpreting the signals or pushing too hard, thus hurting business relationships.

Case Study: Western Company Expanding into South Korea A Western technology company was having poor results with its expansion into South Korea because it could not secure partnerships with local firms. The executives of the firm negotiated in a very direct way, which was perceived as aggressive by the Korean executives, who used indirect, less intrusive communication. Key deals fell through due to perceived cultural insensitivity.

Business Etiquette and Cultural Norms

Something as frivolous as the giving of gifts, exchange of business cards, or seating in meetings would say much between nations such as China and Japan. Any startup that does not attend to such practices is going to inadvertently affront some potential partner or investor and will then lose out on an important deal.

Such cross-cultural misunderstandings could be avoided through proper research, hiring local talents, and partnering with cultural advisors who bridge the gaps between foreign startups and local markets.

Best Practices to Navigate Cultural and Social Factors in Asia

Cultural and social barriers can be overcome with due deliberation and strategy. Startups that invest in learning about local cultures and in relationship-building are most likely to succeed. Best practices include the following:

Cultural Awareness Training

Every startup that decides to enter into any Asian market should invest in cultural awareness training for leadership and teams. Such training and education would point toward possible cultural pitfalls and strategies on how to navigate through local business practices.

Local Talent

The most effective way to bridge cultural gaps may be through bringing local talents on board. Locally hired employees would know all about social norms and business etiquette in their home markets and might prove quite helpful in providing insights related to consumers' reactions and relationship management.

Adapt Business Models to Local Contexts

The startups would make a big mistake simply transplanting a Western business model into Asia. In every market, product and service offerings, as well as business strategies, need to adapt to local contexts of culture and society.

Building Long-Term Relationships

The art of building trust and credibility takes time in any Asian country. It is long-term relationships with partners, investors, and customers that take precedence over the short-term gains that startups need to focus on.

Engage Cultural Advisors

Similarly, a startup can avoid common cultural mistakes and deal with complex social dynamics by engaging with cultural advisors or consultants who have expertise in the local market.

Cultural and social factors are significant in determining the success of startups in Asia. This may range from an understanding of the intricacies of Guanxi and the concept of face to an understanding of hierarchical leadership and ways of avoiding cultural misunderstandings; the startup has to be so equipped to handle these challenges. Investing in cultural awareness, hiring local talent, and adapting business models to suit local contexts will help build stronger and more resilient businesses in Asia for startups. Learning from the previous cultural faux pas and best practices will help them do well in the region's diverse and dynamic markets.

This chapter provides a broad overview of various socio-cultural factors in Asia that may either positively or negatively affect startup success, using real-world case studies and practical strategies to overcome such obstacles.

CHAPTER 12: FOUNDER AND TEAM PSYCHOLOGY BURDENS

Behind every successful start-up are driven founders and dynamic teams, but the human ingredient often gets lost in the formula as perhaps the single biggest determinant of start-up success. In Asia, where cultural pressures are strong, societal expectations run high, and the business environment is relatively risk-averse, these founders and teams commonly face serious psychological challenges. Founder burnout, mental health issues, and lack of team wellbeing have indeed emerged as major factors causing many start-up failures across the region.

This chapter will walk through the psychological toll of Asian entrepreneurship on founders and teams, from the pressure of fast growth and investor expectations to cultural barriers around mental health. Second, we will discuss the importance of fostering a "fail fast, learn faster" mentality in risk-averse cultures and how founders lead with empathy and resilience. Aside from case studies, this chapter has brought out best practices on how startups can encourage founder wellbeing, high-performing teams, and a healthy work culture with regard to mental health.

Founder Burnout and Its Impact on Startup Performance

All that pressure to succeed can wear founders down, leading to burnout—a state of chronic stress and exhaustion. In Asia, where long work hours and cultural expectations around endurance are part and parcel of daily life, founder burnout is a particularly crucial issue. Founders often bear responsibility not only for the strategic vision of the business but also for its day-to-day operations, fundraising, and team dynamics management.

Case Study: Burnout of a Fintech Founder in India

Working on a 100-hour week for years just to satisfy investors and scale up the business took a heavy toll on the burnout levels of the founder of one of India's promising fintech startups. In short, with no very good way out to distribute his responsibilities and take breaks, his health started deteriorating, which eventually led to paralysis in making decisions and decreasing the performance of the company.

- Burnout negatively impacts a founder's capabilities for creative thinking, sane decision-making, and leading clearly. Longer-term, this might lead to poor choices in strategy, dejected morale among the team, and in extreme cases, the closure of the business. Of course, sometimes such pressure to keep high growth rates adds to burnout since most founders sacrifice long-term sustainability for short-term gains.

Early detection and seeking help are necessary to identify the signs that founders are going into burnout. Burnout can be avoided if responsibilities are delegated, care for personal fitness is considered, and the goals set for the mission are practical. This would make sure that burnout does not hinder the growth and development of a startup.

Mental Health Challenges in High-Pressure Startup Environments

Mental health, therefore, goes mostly unnoticed or is stigmatized in most high-pressure environments, especially in startups. This is very much true in Asia, where talking about one's mental health is considered taboo in most societies. However, the stress that accompanies a startup life can be a great cause for serious mental health problems, including anxiety, depression, and emotional exhaustion.

Cultural Barriers to Addressing Mental Health

Many Asian cultures view mental health as a weakness, particularly in the workplace. The fear of losing face or not being able to handle pressure makes founders and employees reluctant to seek help. These issues are further exacerbated by the high level of societal expectations placed on success in countries such as Japan, South Korea, and China, which leads quite often to mental health crises.

Case Study: Anxiety and Depression of the Tech Founder in Japan

A tech startup founder in Tokyo, Japan, suffered from severe anxiety and depression after continuously being defeated in funding rounds. The stigma associated with mental health led the founder to choose silence until his condition worsened. Eventually, this led to the death of the start-up because he could not continue running the company anymore.

Minimizing mental health challenges at a startup requires an open and supportive work environment. Access to mental health resources, taking time off without judgment, and talking openly about the pressures of start-up life can ease the risks associated with mental health.

The Psychological Toll of Failure in Risk-Averse Cultures

In many Asian societies, failure has a strong psychological sting for both founders and employees. In fact, cultural attitudes toward failure in countries like Japan, South Korea, and China often mirror deep-seated feelings of shame and loss of face. For the founders of startups, this means that the prospect of failure is one entailing not only professional failure but even personal and social failure.

Impact of Risk-Aversion on Innovation

The culture and mostly family and society around them shying away from risk habituates startups in Asia to be risk-averse. This, therefore, dampens innovation since founders are wary of trying new ideas or pivoting from business models that do not work for fear of failure. In countries like Japan, for example, where failure is deemed socially destructive, founders take very scanty steps when bold ones are called for in innovation.

Case Study: Cultural Resistance to Failure in South Korea
As a result of the immense societal and familial pressures regarding success, when one first start-up was already struggling to thrive, this South Korean founder brought deep shame. Instead of taking it as an opportunity to learn from his experiences, the founder was highly apprehensive of further judgment and rejection, so he remained out of the entrepreneurial scene for a number of years.

Here, too, more innovation could be stimulated by embracing a "fail fast, learn faster" attitude. That would mean fostering a culture where one is able to view one's failures as part of the deal in becoming an entrepreneur, rather than personal defeat, and would facilitate more risk and more innovation.

Building Cohesive Teams and Promoting Wellbeing

While founders bear enormous pressures, startup teams can also be burned out, and suffer from mental health issues, and dysfunction. In fiercely competitive markets like Asia, talent is hard to hire, and keeping a motivated and aligned team is the most crucial determinant of success. Yet, extremely high levels of turnover, long work hours, and misunderstandings across cultures can stretch team cohesion to a breaking point and lead to disengagement and underperformance.

Team Wellbeing and Leadership

The leadership style of the founders affects the well-being of a team. In many Asian countries, the hierarchical style of leadership creates closed communication, which closes any avenues leading to collaboration. That is, startups are more focused on building inclusive forms of leadership where team members feel empowered to share ideas and concerns, hence improving overall well-being and team dynamics.

Case Study: Talent Retention Challenges in Southeast Asia
A fast-growing e-commerce startup in Southeast Asia faced immense problems retaining its top talents due to burnout and cultural clashes between the local employee base and international management. In that respect, the company desperately had to rethink its approach toward team building by fostering an inclusive work culture appreciating diverse points of view, and taking good care of employee wellbeing problems right from the outset.

In cultivating team wellbeing, a startup should focus on developing a healthy work-life balance, encouraging open communications, and investing in activities that build camaraderie within the team. Regular feedback, recognition of employees, and fostering awareness about mental health will go a long way in building resilience within the team.

Best Practices for Supporting Founder Wellbeing and Building Resilient Teams

Founders' and teams' psychological well-being is important for the eventual success of any startup. Paying attention to mental health, and nurturing positive work conditions, are some of the ways startups can reduce the risk of burnout, high turnover, and dysfunction within the team. Best practices include the following:

Work-Life Balance

Founded on the basis of work-life balance, taking regular time off, and setting boundaries around when one is working versus not. In that regard, founders have to set an example for their own well-being so the organization will take things seriously.

Open Communication

It is one thing to establish a culture of open communication and transparency, which may be done as early as possible. Such activities can be carried out with periodic check-ins, feedback loops, and awareness campaigns on mental health.

Responsibilities Delegation

Most of the founders find it very difficult to delegate responsibilities within firms. This easily results in excessive workload and causes stress or burnout among the founders. Building a leadership team that can share the burden of decision-making and operations is key to preventing founder fatigue.

Psychological Safety

Teams need to have that psychological safety—that feel free to take risks and admit mistakes without fear of retribution. Trust and respect breed innovation, allowing a team to recover from a setback without the loss of morale.

Access to Mental Health Resources

Startups should offer access to resources such as counseling services, wellness programs, and workshops on stress management. By allowing and encouraging employees to use these resources, a much healthier environment can be established.

The human element plays a pivotal role in the fortunes of startups in Asia. From founder burnout and mental health to poor team dynamics, it's almost a never-ending list as to what can bring down even the most promising of ventures. By fostering a culture that prioritizes mental health, open communication, and resilience, startups can create an environment in which founders and teams alike can thrive. Embracing the fact that failure forms part of the learning curve, well-being, and putting in place strong, cohesive teams will support these startups through the ruthless pressures that come with entrepreneurship in building sustainable and successful businesses.

CHAPTER 13: BUILD PROFITABLE ASIAN STARTUPS

The rare combination indeed requires innovation, cultural adaptability, financial discipline, and strong leadership to succeed and build resilient startups in Asia. The reasons for the failures of so many Asian startups-from misaligned business models and regulatory challenges to leadership failures and mental health crises-have been discussed in previous chapters. This chapter synthesizes those insights and provides actionable strategies to help entrepreneurs negotiate the unique complexity presented by the Asian startup ecosystem.

This final chapter explores how startups can learn from past failures, build resilient business models, establish an innovative culture, and scale globally-facing sustainable ventures. Future trends and emerging opportunities are also included in the discussion on this dynamic Asian startup landscape. With the correct mindset and approach, entrepreneurs can rise not only above the challenges that faced earlier startups but also furthered the region's growing influence on the global stage.

Failures to Teach Resilience

While failure is greatly stigmatized in many Asian cultures, for entrepreneurs, it is just one aspect of their journey. Learning from failure and changing track becomes so important for long-term success at startups. Asian entrepreneurs will have to adopt the "fail fast, learn faster" mentality; indeed, setbacks will be crucial to teaching key lessons for growth and innovation in the future.

Case Study: How Go-Jek Adapted in Indonesia

The initial struggle of Go-Jek in the ride-hailing market was what made the firm adapt quickly into a super-app offering food delivery to digital payment services. Learned from initial difficulties, Go-Jek grew to become one of the most fortunate tech startups in Indonesia through the expansion of its ecosystem while standing tall in a highly competitive environment.

The Value of Failure

Learning from failure; doing honest post-mortems after setbacks to understand the root causes of the failure and make the necessary adjustments to their business models and strategies. Iterating on such lessons helps more startups ride out the volatile startup landscape.

This helps a startup be resilient and effective at innovating by fostering a culture that sees failure as an opportunity to learn, not a defeat personally or professionally.

Creating Robust yet Adaptive Business Models

An essential ingredient for building a successful startup would be to develop a sound, flexible business model aligned with the market realities. Asian startups have a myriad of cases where business models are misaligned owing to the tendency for over-dependence on Western frameworks that fail to localize offerings meant for diverse and fragmented markets across the region. Startups, when developing business models, would need to emphasize scalability and agility in order to adapt to changing market conditions.

Market Fit and Localization

It would be important that startups focus on the business models that fit the local market in order to meet specific market needs. For example, Southeast Asian consumers' habits of purchasing may be different from those of East Asia consumers when it comes to means of paying for services. Only then will companies whose products, services, and business strategies are attuned to the local contexts likely be successful.

Revenue and Sustainability

Most of these startups chase growth at the expense of profitability, hence unsustainable burn rates. Instead, the building of sustainable revenue models should be an early focus of the startups through focused efforts toward profitability and long-term financial health. To make such decisions that would result in practicality and operations, indeed, there is a need for tight and firm knowledge concerning market demand, strategies of pricing, and competition.

Thus, it serves a particular focus on adaptability and sustainability that will keep the startups strong against market fluctuations and economic turmoil.

Creating a Culture of Experimentation and Innovation

Innovation might be at the core of any successful startup, but in the competitive markets of Asia, nurturing an attitude of experimentation has become the key to moving forward. Those startups that give priority to continuous innovation tend to stay at the front in identifying fresh opportunities for growth, hence keeping themselves from stagnation.

Experiments encouraged

Grab and Tokopedia are prime examples of successful startups because experimentation was encouraged through the incorporation of a continuous trial of new ideas, products, and services. Give their employees the ability to be innovative and take calculated risks. They know that all the experiments won't succeed, but the information it produce is gold.

Emerging Technologies for Competitive Advantage

Emerging technologies in AI, blockchain, and the Internet of Things will provide competitive advantages through innovation. These technologies can be put to use by Asian startups, but particularly in industries such as fintech, e-commerce, and logistics, in order to solve complex local problems that range from financial inclusion to supply chain optimization.

Case Study: Innovation ecosystem at Alibaba
Alibaba has been able to create an innovation ecosystem through heavy investments in AI and big data to continuously improve its e-commerce platform, logistics operations, and financial services. This continuous innovation has helped the company stay ahead of its competition in a very aggressive market.

Encouraging experimentation, adoption of new technologies, and fostering a mindset of continuous improvement will help the startups stay lean yet responsive to the market needs.

Creating Global-Facing, Sustainable Startups

Though several Asian startups have focused on either the local or regional market, there is growing pressure to build globally competitive businesses. To that effect, startups targeting international expansion must forge global-facing strategies right from the outset, factoring in unique challenges and opportunities brought forth by this global scale of operation.

Global Market Readiness

Competing at an international level, Asian Startups must make products and services to meet the tastes and preferences of the end consumer, regulatory requirements, and competitive landscapes prevalent across other regions. Successful startups on the global scene understand how to adapt their offerings to different cultural contexts without losing a unified brand and vision.

Sustainability for Competitive Advantage

In the current world, sustainability has become an increasingly important factor for startups. This can be developed as a differential advantage for Asian startups, incorporating business practices of sustainable reduction of carbon footprint, ethical supply chains, and investing in green technologies. Nowadays, sustainability plays a great role both in the world of consumers and investors; taking up environmental and social responsibility will give the edge to startups in the global market.

Case Study: Grab's regional and global expansion

Grab continued its relentless expansion outside of Southeast Asia into new areas. Most recently attempted financial services, digital payment, and ride-hailing in several markets. Grab is able to localize the offering while having a scalable platform to accommodate new markets.

Paying attention to global-facing strategies and sustainability can help startups create resilient businesses that are poised for long-term success on the world stage.

Mentorship, Ecosystem Support, and Forward-Looking Mindsets

Each successful startup is not an island unto itself but is greatly helped by good mentorship, access to a supportive ecosystem, and cultivating a forward-looking mindset that fosters continuous learning and collaboration.

The Role of Mentorship

Mentorship helps startups gain the necessary guidance and insight to overcome obstacles and make sound decisions. Experienced mentors can provide recommendations pertaining to strategy, fundraising, scaling, and leadership to founders in order to circumvent common missteps. Mentoring networks also extend to the ecosystems in Singapore, China, and India that link entrepreneurs with industry veterans, venture capitalists, and corporate leaders.

Ecosystem Support

Supportive ecosystems, incubators, accelerators, and government-supported initiatives remain important to support the creation of startup ventures. For instance, Singapore and Japan have provided suitable eco-systems via grants, tax incentives, and innovation hubs that equip early-stage startups with the resources they require to scale into success.

Future-Proofing via Education

It is basically adaptation and learning. A startup should always remain one step ahead in terms of industry trends, changes in technology, and changes in the market by investing significantly in founders and team education. Developing a learning culture will definitely keep startups competitive in today's fast-moving business world.

By leveraging mentorship, supportive ecosystems, and building a culture of continuous learning, startups can create a tending of their networks and knowledge so vital to long-term success.

Building the Future of Asian Startups

The future for Asian startups lies in the process of building robust, adaptable, and globally competitive businesses. Learning from failure, innovating, following sustainable business models, and encouraging a culture of experimentation are ways to help guide startups through the gauntlet of complexities in the vibrant Asian market toward international success. Mentorship and ecosystem support, besides having a forward-looking mindset, are but a must in future-proofing the startups that would enable them to seize emerging opportunities and further grow Asia's influence in the global startup ecosystem. If equipped with appropriate strategies and a mindset to do so, startups in Asia have the potential to shape the future of entrepreneurship within the region and worldwide.

ACKNOWLEDGEMENT

In creating this book, I have been extraordinarily fortunate to draw upon the wisdom and expertise of an exceptional global network of partners and friends. Their contributions, both direct and indirect, have profoundly shaped this work, and I am deeply grateful for their influence. The following deserve special acknowledgements:

Kanth Krishnan, Managing Director at Accenture, whose visionary leadership and penetrating insights in technology services have been truly inspiring. His deep industry knowledge has substantially enriched this book's content.

Jeff Pappas, Managing Director at Newmark, who offered vital perspectives on the global real estate market landscape, bringing unmatched expertise to our exploration of diverse business environments.

Haitao Qi, Chairman of Devott Research and Advisory, whose illuminating insights on technology innovations and market trends, particularly in Asia, have been invaluable.

Charles Aird, former head of Outsourcing and Managed Services at PwC, whose comprehensive knowledge and strategic vision in outsourcing services have deeply informed my understanding of this crucial business function.

Mike Beares, Founder and Board Chairman of Clutch.co, whose entrepreneurial vision and commitment to connecting businesses with optimal service providers have significantly influenced my perspective on business connectivity.

Marc Schwarz, an industry pioneer in technology services, global sourcing, and innovation since the 1980s. His distinguished career spanning PwC, Deloitte, HP, and Sun Microsystems has yielded insights that have transformed our clients' businesses.

The merits of this book are a direct reflection of this exceptional global network, while any shortcomings are entirely my own responsibility.

Finally, I must express my deepest gratitude to my wife, Biyu, whose unwavering support and understanding have been fundamental to this endeavor. The intensive writing process, reminiscent of my doctoral dissertation at Yale twenty-five years ago, was made possible by her continuous encouragement. She remains the driving force behind both my professional growth and personal fulfillment.

ABOUT THE AUTHOR

Stephan S. Sunn

Stephan Sunn serves as Executive Partner at Sanford Black Advisory, a leading global business and investment consultancy. He advises companies worldwide on growth strategy, marketing and sales optimization, innovation monetization, strategic partnerships, and mergers & acquisitions. Co-founding Davidson Global & Co. with partners from premier consulting firms and technology companies, Stephan works to make high-quality consulting services more affordable and accessible to startups and SMEs globally.

Over two decades, he has led 120+ corporate consulting engagements, advised 48 cities and technology parks, and collaborated with 500+ service providers. His portfolio spans 50+ international marketing projects, 20+ M&A transactions, and 40+ global events across technology services sectors. Stephan holds a honorary leadership role at Devott Co., China's foremost private research firm in IT and technology services, and serves as a Director of the China IT and Outsourcing Association. His clients range from Fortune 500 corporations to startups in both developed and emerging markets.

A graduate of the University of Science and Technology of China (USTC) with a Bachelor of Science degree, and Yale University with both Master of Science and Ph.D., Stephan is a frequent speaker at global conferences and a prolific author in his professional fields.

BOOKS BY THIS AUTHOR

Competing For The Growth: How Cities And Technology Parks Attract Global Trades And Investments

This book serves as a guidebook for city planners, economic development professionals, tech park builders, and public officials who aim to create thriving innovation communities that attract global trade and stimulate investments. It offers a structured path that begins with intangible factors like vision setting and partnership alignment and extends to pilots and full-blown magnet programs.

The book provides real-life instructions to help put these ideas into practice, including effective strategies for attracting rapidly growing businesses and talent, creating a setting that promotes innovation and entrepreneurship, fostering a competitive and appealing business climate, and building a globally recognized brand and reputation.

The author emphasizes that cities and tech parks must play to their strengths and assets to compete and win in the global arena. The race for relevance is on, and the window of opportunity to determine the outcome is closing. Cities and companies have what they need to succeed, and with the options, relationships, and guidance provided in this book, city managers and tech park authorities can make the decisions necessary to lead their communities to success in the world investment and trade arena.

Searching The New Profits: How The US SMEs And Startups Succeed In The

Emerging Markets

In the face of global market turbulence and domestic uncertainties, American small and medium-sized businesses (SMBs) and startups have significant growth opportunities in emerging markets. However, these markets also present unique challenges. This handbook provides a semi-analytical and semi-prescriptive approach to help American SMBs and entrepreneurs succeed in these rapidly expanding markets. Conversely, governments, technology parks, and corporations in emerging countries can utilize this book to learn how to collaborate with U.S. companies in their markets to serve their customers effectively.

The book covers essential themes such as researching and identifying matching markets, choosing the appropriate market entry mode, local marketing and sales tactics, effective risk management, establishing an active and reputable presence in the local market, ensuring full legal compliance, avoiding political involvement, talent search and retention, and balancing standardization and localization. The final chapter shares valuable lessons from decades of business practices, acknowledging that readers may have different perspectives on these topics. Expanding knowledge through diverse viewpoints is beneficial for U.S. SMB and startup leaders. Despite the challenges, penetrating foreign markets can be highly profitable, and U.S. enterprises have a reasonable chance of success by capitalizing on the vast potential of these rapidly growing territories.

Cracking The Winning Codes: How Global Vendors Win In The US Digital And Outsourcing Markets

This book serves as a comprehensive guide for international technology and outsourcing companies seeking to enter and succeed in the highly competitive U.S. market. It emphasizes the importance of adapting to the unique American business culture, which values innovation, diversity, relationships, customer-centricity, and results-oriented management. The guide highlights the need to navigate the complex U.S. regulatory landscape, including federal and state laws, as well as key legislations such as FCPA, SOX, and HIPAA.

The book covers essential topics such as understanding American business culture, complying with legal requirements, developing effective marketing strategies, employing successful sales techniques, addressing cultural differences, and managing risks associated with entering a new market. Additionally, it encourages the use of innovative tactics to differentiate from competitors and gain market share.

A special section titled "The Lessons" shares the author's personal experiences and insights, providing practical execution tips that focus on solution-oriented approaches, leveraging referrals and testimonials, managing communication costs, delivering higher quality than promised, and investing in proven local sales leaders.

By adhering to the core principles of understanding buyer preferences, continuous innovation, human capital development, risk management, customer-centricity, and resilient operations, global providers can successfully navigate and thrive in the lucrative U.S. market.

Win More Deals In The Digital Era
How Martech And Salestech Improve Marketing And Sales

In the new economy, businesses must navigate the complex landscape of Marketing Technology (Martech) and Sales Technology (Salestech) to stay competitive and drive growth. "Win More Deals in Digital Age" provides a comprehensive guide for leveraging these technologies to enhance customer experiences, streamline processes, and boost revenue across international markets.

The book explores the convergence of marketing, sales, and technology, emphasizing the importance of data-driven decision-making and cross-functional collaboration. It offers strategies for overcoming challenges in digital transformation, such as resistance to change and skills gaps, while also addressing the unique considerations of global expansion and localization. The authors predict future trends in Martech and Salestech, including the increasing role of AI, personalization, and emerging technologies like AR/VR and voice interfaces. Through real-world success stories from global brands like Coca-Cola, Sephora, and Airbnb, readers gain valuable insights into harnessing the power of these technologies for business success. This book serves as an essential resource for executives and professionals seeking to navigate the digital ecosystem and drive growth in the international marketplace.

Renovations Or Revolutions: Impacts Of Latest AI On BPO And Contact Centers

The book "Renovation or Revolution? Impacts of Latest AI on BPO and Contact-centers Industries" provides an in-depth exploration of the transformative potential of artificial intelligence (AI) within the business process outsourcing (BPO) and contact center industries. It emphasizes the importance of early adoption, customization, and localization of AI solutions to gain a competitive edge in the global marketplace. The book highlights the evolving role of human agents, who will focus on complex problem-solving and relationship-building, while AI handles routine tasks. It also discusses the development of AI expertise within organizations and the ethical considerations surrounding AI implementation.

The authors present a roadmap for incorporating AI, underlining the need for a clear vision, employee training, and continuous improvement. Looking ahead, the book envisions a future of collaborative human-AI partnerships, hyper-personalization, and proactive customer engagement. It stresses that embracing AI is crucial for BPO and contact center companies to achieve sustainable growth and remain competitive in the international arena. The book serves as a comprehensive guide for executives navigating the AI revolution in the global business services industry.

Risky Reefs In The Ocean Of Global Markets: Common Mistakes Emerging Markets' Companies In Their Global Expansions

This book provides a comprehensive roadmap for emerging market companies venturing into global expansion. It highlights common pitfalls across strategic planning, finance, operations, human resources, marketing, technology, legal/ethics, and risk management. The book emphasizes thorough market research, cultural adaptation, local partnerships, brand building, innovation investment, and long-term vision.

As the global landscape evolves, it anticipates trends like digitization, sustainability integration, and talent acquisition challenges. The book provides corporate decision-makers with insights and best practices to navigate complexities, mitigate risks, and foster sustainable growth while driving innovation and progress internationally.

The AI Revolution In B2B Marketing And Sales: Disruptions Of AI In The Conventional B2B Markets

This professional guidance provides a comprehensive playbook for leveraging artificial intelligence (AI) to drive measurable results in B2B marketing and sales strategies. With insights from real-world case studies spanning diverse industries and business sizes, it explores AI's transformative impact on understanding the AI-empowered buyer, delivering personalized omnichannel experiences, boosting sales productivity, and optimizing operations.

The book offers a strategic framework for successful AI implementation, covering data readiness, talent acquisition, governance, and ethical considerations. Globally applicable principles foster human-AI collaboration, enabling organizations worldwide to harness AI's potential ethically and profitably in the B2B domain.

Promotor, Suppressor Or Neutralizer Impact Of Latest AI And Geopolitics On Global Outsourcing

This book explores how artificial intelligence (AI) and geopolitics are transforming the global outsourcing industry. It analyzes the strategic implications of AI for outsourcing operations, delivery models, talent management, and client relationships. The impact of geopolitical forces like trade tensions, political instability, and regulatory shifts on risk mitigation and geographic diversification is examined.

Emerging business models combining AI and human expertise, niche services, innovation through collaboration, workforce upskilling, and ethical AI governance are highlighted. The book provides a strategic roadmap for international outsourcing providers to navigate challenges, seize opportunities, and drive sustainable growth in this era of technological disruption and evolving geopolitical dynamics.

Pricing For Profitability And Growth: Mastering Pricing Strategies In Technology And Services Globally

This book explores how companies in the technology and service sectors can leverage strategic pricing to drive growth and profitability. It advocates moving beyond traditional cost-plus pricing to adopt value-based approaches that align pricing with customer perceptions of value. Key recommendations include: conducting thorough market research to understand customer needs and willingness to pay; segmenting customers and offering differentiated pricing tiers; leveraging data and analytics for dynamic pricing optimization; and aligning sales, marketing and pricing teams around a cohesive value proposition. The book emphasizes the importance of quantifying and communicating value to justify premium pricing.
Looking to the future, the book highlights how artificial intelligence and machine learning will transform pricing capabilities, enabling more personalized and responsive pricing strategies. It cautions against common

pitfalls like failing to account for competitive responses or neglecting the psychology of pricing. Ultimately, the authors argue that pricing is a critical strategic capability that requires ongoing experimentation, cross-functional collaboration, and a willingness to adapt to changing market conditions. By taking a customer-centric, data-driven approach to pricing, technology and service companies can gain a powerful lever for sustainable growth and competitive advantage.

GovTech, Governance Technology: Unlocking Competitive Advantage For Cities And Tech Parks

This book dives into GovTech's potential to revolutionize government and urban development. By leveraging data, AI, and e-government platforms, GovTech can streamline processes, boost transparency, and even enhance citizen engagement. The book emphasizes collaboration between government, businesses, academia, and citizens to create a thriving GovTech ecosystem. Success stories from Estonia and Singapore showcase how GovTech can attract investment, streamline business operations, and fuel economic growth. Furthermore, the book explores GovTech's role in fostering innovation hubs and simplifying business registrations, particularly for SMEs. It also delves into the power of data-driven governance and AI to transform public services and policymaking. Finally, the human aspect is crucial. Building a skilled workforce, managing cultural shifts, and promoting digital literacy are all emphasized for GovTech to reach its full potential.

www.ingramcontent.com/pod-product-compliance
Lightning Source LLC
Chambersburg PA
CBHW070422240526
45472CB00020B/1147